PINTEREST MARKETING

80K TO 14+ MILLION IN 3 MONTHS

KERRIE LEGEND

kerrie
LEGEND
pinterest expert | designer | blogger | author

CONTENTS

PREFACE

There are over 75 billion ideas on Pinterest.

Average time spent on Pinterest per visit is 14.2 minutes.

87% of Pinners have purchased a product because of Pinterest.

ACKNOWLEDGMENTS

To my children - stay inspired, color, plan, build,
and most importantly, dream.
Pinterest will help.

FOREWORD

In December 2018, I took a chance. I buckled down, focused, and was determined to grow my blog in an exponential way. I had been using Pinterest and teaching its principles and my methods for about two years, but had never reached the point of dominating this platform.

At the beginning of December, I had 80k monthly viewers on Pinterest. Three months later, I had increased traffic and revenue on my blog by over 400k page views, and approximately 60k user sessions.

By February, I had conquered Pinterest.

But more importantly, what I discovered in those three months of focused improvement and growth was that my methods were able to be replicated no matter the niche, the size of the account, or even age of the account.

At the end, I detail what I did to grow to 14 million monthly views, with over 450k of those visitors coming to my blog regularly, as well as how my email list grew by around 30k in the process.

You can do this, too. I know you can. I've outlined everything you need to know and have gone into detail on how to make blogging one of the most joyous, prosperous activities you can do. Drama free, with a reach beyond anything you'll get with social media.

This is an exciting book for those of you that want free website traffic and to build your follower base. This book has been created, cultivated, and modified from my course, and if you'd like to take the full course to get the full aspect of all the software including screen prints and discussion, you're encouraged to do just that.

The course is available for purchase on my website at kerrielegend.com. The Pinterest course covers everything in this book and more. Everything you could possibly want to know about Pinterest is included in this book. I've been told numerous times by pinners that my book and the course are the most comprehensive instruction you will find on the web. That's good news for you, if you're just developing an interest on Pinterest. You're in the right place.

Over 5000 entrepreneurs just like you have taken my Pinterest course as of March 2019. It's been an amazing journey with them all - helping special people with big dreams make them happen. I couldn't be more thrilled. If you'd like to take my course, I'd be happy to have you in my self-paced class, and assist you with anything you need. But if you're good with this book, too, then by all means, read on!

We're going to create some amazing, share-worthy pins and get your website and email list hopping with people!

This book is for everyone interested in Pinterest—it doesn't matter if you're a local business focused on services and want to grow or expand so you can stop trading dollars for hours, or an amazing infopreneur who wants to use Pinterest and learn the strategy to be seen even more. All are welcome! There's a niche market for EVERYONE on Pinterest. And if you don't see your specialty on Pinterest just yet, well you're in luck - you're about to corner the market! :)

Let's get started!

1 ESTABLISH YOUR BLOG'S UNIQUE FOCUS

81% of Pinterest users are actually females.

L et's talk about creating your unique focus when it comes to your blog and the online segment of your business. You might be wondering why we're talking about focus when this book is all about using Pinterest strategies to grow your followers and make a ton of money, but before we even can discuss Pinterest strategies, your foundation needs to be firmed up. Your blog's focus is your all-important foundation. Without a foundation, you have nothing to stand on. So, let's nail down your foundation first to have a firm understanding on how we're going to build your business from there.

Why do we need to hone in on focus? Why do we care so much about focus with Pinterest?

First, if you write about a lot of different things and subjects, it's harder for your readers to grasp onto what exactly you're all about. One day you could be blogging about your favorite website to get ideas from and the next it might be about something that recently happened in the news. Perhaps you gained followers over your post about new ideas but they don't like reading about current events on your blog. You'll lose followers and interest in what you have to say if you're bouncing around on topics.

Think about this as you would an activity such as reading the newspaper. You probably have favorite sections that you read the most, right? Most people don't have time to read an entire newspaper front to back, and even if they do, they probably have their "favorites". They might enjoy the business section or even the arts section. Your blog operates in the same fashion. You want your blog to be that specific section of the newspaper they love and open every single day, and have them dying to read more of what you might share with them. If you think of the newspaper and your blog in that way, you can better understand the concept of developing a focus area, also known as a niche in some circles.

We can't assume that we can get away with writing about tons of different topics because newspapers are a whole different ballgame. We're individual bloggers, for the most part, and do not have the manpower to even take on such a task. But, as a single entrepreneur blogger, we can certainly focus in on one subject or concept and run with that.

Cater, in a way, to the person that loves a particular section of a newspaper. We want them coming back day after day to read. You already have them interested, so don't blow it! If you're writing about tons of different topics, then you make it hard for people to really grasp onto your site and love every single thing that you put out there. Sure, there will be posts that resonate with your audience more than others, and it's It also gives you the chance to connect with your readers consistently rather than having some readers who like your articles about cocktails and appetizers and those that like your posts about Instagram tips.

You really want to create readers who love **everything** that you do. You don't want to them to have to sift through your posts just to find something that they enjoy reading, so maybe they really like your tips on Instagram, but it's not worth it to them to have to come to your blog every day and hope there is a new cocktail image and drink to try out but then end up waiting for who knows how long for another one to show up on your blog or feed.

Consistency is the name of the game with establishing your focus. You'll want to be consistent in your focus so that you give your readers what they crave to read and looking for every single time they visit your blog. No surprises unless it's a bonus download!

Here's the kicker. If they visit your blog from Pinterest, they probably liked what they clicked over to read, but they're probably not going to be interested in all those other topics you cover. I didn't just create this book to bring a ton of traffic to your site. I don't want to just create random visitors to your blog or your website, I want to help you create fans of your site and your writing; people who love what you're doing and are going to stick around for the long haul. The strategies, goals and tasks in this book will work by bringing lots of new traffic to your site, but it is so up to you to create a defined focus in order to keep them around and coming back for more.

Let's look at a scenario...

Many people, including major brands, have not developed a solid understanding of how Pinterest can really work. It's a search engine tool—not a social media platform. Therefore, you're pinning things that people might search for and want to try.

At first, people developed hodge-podge boards with all sorts of things. Maybe they would sort them out with "things to try" or "goals for 2017". For the non-business user, it's perfectly fine to do it that way. But for a business or blogger, that's not the best way to approach Pinterest. So now, I'm teaching entrepreneurs a new way to handle Pinterest to make it work for your blog and business, regardless of what kind it is. So let's take a look at a scenario so I can show you exactly what I mean.

If you've ever been to one of my online classes, you might have heard this scenario before, but it's relevant and I'm going to share it here again because I think it defines and describes why it is so important to have a focus in an easy to understand way.

Imagine two blogs in front of you in separate browsers. The blow in the first browser (we'll call it Blog 1) is a cute, well-designed millennial pink blog that talks about all sorts of things: fashion, shoes, pets, interior design, gift ideas, cocktails, relationships, self-development, etc. There are a ton of subject areas and that's typically what you'd find in a lifestyle blog. Blog 2 is a blog about home woman-caves and man-caves—designing them, building them, and styling for them.

Let's say you see a pin on Pinterest that has the title "Interior Design Tips for Woman-caves". If this pin leads you to Blog 1, (remember this is the blog that has a ton of different topics), then you're going to love it. You're looking for ideas to make your own home getaway area—something you crave so you can lock the door and escape the kiddos for an hour!

Let's say you're really interested in learning more about design ideas for woman-caves. You find the post useful. You'll probably start browsing around for more information on the same thing just to get second opinions or even more style ideas, right? But, wait. There's information on the latest gift Blogger 1 found for her best friend forever, a cocktail recipe, her latest breakup advice and finding the right man, etc. Then you start seeing posts and pins for her cosmetic business with links to an online store than has nothing to do with interior design. OH, and then there are posts and pins about her skinny wrap business and immediately, you're like, blah! It's not relevant to what you're interested in!

Now if the same pin leads to Blog 2, remember it is the exact same article, then you'll love the post—same as before. It's so useful and you crave more information! You'll have the same reaction and start perusing the Blog 2. You realize you just hit a goldmine of interior cave-building. Not only is there a free style guide and list of shopping items to collect for your new cave at home, but there is a collection of pictures and ideas that you can save to your pin board to show your spouse or partner for later. And even better, Blog 2 has a few things you can buy right off of the site and it'll ship first thin in the morning. How reliable! That's really how you build a foundation to sell products to your audience and grow as a blogger or business.

Because Blog 2 is building that foundation where they are setting themselves apart as an expert in interior design for man-caves and woman-caves (aka she-caves), you'll come back to the site for more... knowing that it's reliable for what your goal is. You'll probably go back to it a few more times, maybe even make a purchase or two, sign up for the newsletter or mailing list, or visit often to get new, inspired ideas.

Now when you narrow your focus, you create content that your ideal audience can consume, rather than have to sift through tons of articles that are irrelevant to them. Remember—our goals as bloggers and businesses is to provide for an audience—our blogs and busi-nesses are not about our own preferences or ourselves. They're going to go through a ton of other articles on your site and find a lot of similar and useful information that is relevant to them. You are going to become the go-to hub for a certain topic or niche.

This is super-simple and easy.

I think a lot of people really want to become the go-to hub or a more popular, more prestigious blogger. They want to have influence and make big sales. There's nothing wrong with that - and it is not that hard if you have a strong focus on your blog. People will start to turn to you and assume that you are a leader and an expert in that particular niche.

The problem is that so many people try to cover tons of different topics and it makes it really hard for them to stand out. So, you're going to need to set yourself apart as a leader and expert in a certain subject. You're also going to build an audience that trusts you, visits your work often and would likely buy from you. Wonderful, right? That's exactly what you want! It's the perfect outcome. It can only really happen if you narrow your focus, though.

For myself, for example, I've set myself apart from the pack by focusing on developing strategies through writing and design. People visit kerrielegend.com to see my articles because they see my growth, the productivity, and want to know more about how they, too, can be productive and develop a strategy that works for them.

How do you find your focus ?

We talked about why focus is so important. Now how do you find it? A formula if you will: your passion and talent plus how you can help or serve people, equals your focus. It's not exactly scientific by any means, but it works. Your passion and talent, so whatever you are good at, what you love doing, plus how you can use that passion and talent to serve other people, is your focus.

Taking me as an example, my talent is in design and writing sales copy through developing a social media strategy. That's my talent and that's my passion. I love creating graphics and showing people how to grow as well. So how I help is by teaching others design tips and social media strategy. So that's my focus; I focus on helping business owners and bloggers grow through social media channels. Your focus is so important because it is what is going to set you apart from the rest of the pack. Having a strong focus and a clear audience will make your work more memorable, shareable and profitable. You are abso-lutely going to win at blogging if you learn Pinterest.

I used to blog about goats and goat milk. It was what I did on our farm so I figured I could develop a niche around that. But guess what?! As much as I love my goats and farm and all the benefits they bring from a health standpoint, goats and goat's milk was not my passion. My own blog used to be pretty much your standard DIY blog. When I was describing Blog 2 earlier, that was pretty much describing me. I had a niche, and a small audience, but I wasn't passionate enough about it. I wasn't excited about my focus area. My boards had kind of anything that had to do with goats but there was no strategy behind it. I decided to really hone in on my focus which is sharing design, social media and entrepreneurial advice, and since then, my blog has grown by leaps and bounds.

Your homework

Figure out where your biggest passion and talent intersects with how you can help your audience. Find a way to solve a problem. Get specific about what you offer. Don't just try to think generally; try to think more specifically about what exactly you're going to talk about. Define specific categories, topics, and posts that you will write in order to attract that certain audience and serve them in a really relevant way. Schedule them out so you can start designing your pins straight away.

You could also brainstorm products or services that you can offer, as well. Remember to get specific with your ideas.

Now would be a good time to decide: What do I want to be the go-to hub for? If somebody was writing a blog post titled "My Favorite (fill in the blank) Blogs", maybe you write a baby blog, so "My Favorite Baby Blogs". What do you want to be the go-to hub for? Maybe you are the go-to hub for toy buying advice or style for baby gear. You really want to get specific about what you want to be the go-to hub for, and then just imagine those types of blog posts where somebody is writing about their favorite types of blogs in a certain specific niche and what they would say about your blog. So answer the question: What do you want to be the go-to hub for?

JUST TO RECAP...

• A clear focus will help you stand out and create raving fans, not just one-time followers or visitors, but visitors that will come back for more because they crave what you have to say.

• We don't just want people to click over to your site from Pinterest, we really want them to stick around, so make your website a "play area" for people to discover.

• Your focus is your talent and passion plus how you can serve your audience, so be sure to define what your talents are and what your passion is. Sometimes we are great at doing certain things but that doesn't mean we are passionate about them.

2 LET'S GET STARTED AND DEFINE YOUR TRIBE

40% of new signups are men; 60% new signups are women.

I n this chapter, we're talking about defining your tribe. A tribe is like your online family—they will re-pin your stuff, come see you from time to time if not daily, and be your fans.

Focus plus audience equals love for your blog and business. Tribes help generate that love. Those two things are so important to creating a stellar standout brand; focus and audience. Your focus and your audience go hand-in-hand, and those two things help you define your tribe and find them.

Many people have trouble defining their audience because they don't have a clear focus, so start with your focus and then define your audience based on your focus. Your tribe is waiting for you out there somewhere—so this is not something you want to rush into. It's so much easier to do it that way than to try and think who your audience is when you have an unfocused blog or business. So, start with your focus and then your audience is going to become obvious. The more focused your content is, the easier it will be to define your exact audience. The tribe will follow.

Answer the who question

Who are you blogging for? To create a consistent blog, you need to know who you are creating it for. It's hard to create a consistent blog if you have no idea of who your audience is. Carve out your typical person you would consider as part of your audience. Don't think of your audience as an actual audience, that kind of clumps everybody into this big massive unknown; think of them as one person. This is even better if you know someone who is representative of your ideal audience. Because then you can create everything for that person, and have a litmus test of relevance and whether or not it's relatable. Rather than trying to think if it is going to resonate with an entire audience, you just have one person that you are creating everything for.

If you take the course, there's a workbook, where you have an opportunity to fill out an audience profile and answer some questions that are really going to help you hone in on who your tribe is. It's also going to help you define who that one person you are creating your blog posts for, so really work on that handout, too, because that's going to help you define your tribe and your focus.

Defining your audience

There are three ways to define your audience aside from doing the activities in the handout:

1. One is to ask your audience something: do a survey. If you have even a small audience right now, you can totally do a survey on your blog or your website just to see who your people are. Ask a few questions like where they live, which posts they tend to like the most, etc. Basically, inquire with any questions that are going to give you a good

idea of why they have come to your website. Why do they come to you? What do they think of your blog?

2. Look back through your old content to see what received the most comments. If it has received a lot of comments then it shows that people are engaging with it. What received the most views? If people are viewing it, then obviously they are interested in it. What received any other attention such as the post that was re-tweeted a lot? It's also worth a look to check your Pinterest analytics to see which content does the best on Pinterest. Then you can tell which content you should be creating more of for your audience. (Surprisingly, in addition to my blog posts, my font pins have performed the best! Wow – who knew?!)

3. And then lastly in the handout, creating an audience profile and answering those targeted questions to help you define your audience for your blog or website.

Now, once you know who your audience is, you can create content that they will love. For me, I started making pins and recommending fonts to use for designing social media posts. My pins went wild! My fans love them!

You need to know who your audience and fans are they are so that you can serve them to the best of your ability. Remember, this is not about you, we're not creating a Pinterest or a blog for you, because you are not your audience. You are creating this for all those people, those awesome people who love what you create that will be your tribe. Remember, this isn't about you, this is about them.

The second aspect of the formula

Here's another aspect of a non-scientific formula: your passion and talent plus how you can help or serve people—the last time it amounted to your focus. This time, it equals your content. Basically, it's the same thing, your focus and your content. Your passion, your talent and how you can help or serve people equals your content.

Now, figure out the best content for your people: what problem are you solving for them? For me, it has been helping bloggers who lead busy lives create a time-efficient, productive social media strategy. I pin new fonts to use in their designs to keep things fresh. It works for me. But what works for my audience will not work for yours. So you need to take some time with this question. What's the takeaway that is going to impact their life? Remember, we are making it all about your audience. How are you helping them?

Make it share-worthy; if they wouldn't want to share it then why are you writing it? Don't be afraid to do what others aren't; ignore the competition to an extent. Gary Vaynerchuk has always been an inspiration of mine – he always stresses about not worrying about what others are doing when you're creating. Focus on you and what you can bring to the table. Put your stamp on it.

You don't want to go completely off the grid, but you want to make sure that it is still relevant to your audience. Don't be afraid to do what they are not doing or offering their audience. Don't be afraid to expand on their ideas or to try different medium if nobody else in your niche is doing it. Create the best content for your people so that you are solving their problems and giving them a solid takeaway.

JUST TO RECAP...

• Define your tribe so that you can create content that is exuberantly relevant to them. Keep it fresh and natural, and don't overthink your audience or tribe.

• Figure out what problem you are solving for your audience – ask, listen and implement.

• Understand your audience by doing a survey, researching your old popular content and creating an audience profile by using an ideal person in mind to humanize it a bit.

You can then create content that is very relevant to your followers, so much so that they are going to share and love and pin. In the next chapter, we're going to be talking all about how to create killer content. Now that we know our focus and our audience, we are ready to create some stellar content. So, make sure you also fill out those worksheets in the handout. Those are going to help you a lot in these next few chapters.

3 DEVELOPING KILLER CONTENT

Men account for only 7% of total pins on Pinterest.

As you may imagine, having killer content is a cornerstone of being able to rock it on Pinterest. So is having an amazing website (but that's for another book). In this chapter, we are going to be talking about what goes into creating killer content online and how you can use this strategy to your advantage to grow your brand and following on Pinterest.

Having a focus will get people interested when they arrive on your site, especially if that focus resonates with them, but you need awesome content if you want to keep them around. You can't just have a strong focus but then have bad content where it is not engaging or it's not interesting, or it's not really giving them anything valuable. Having a strong focus and then also having awesome content is important to growing your blog and website.

Like many other platforms, Pinterest has an algorithm. Many people know that great content goes beyond pleasing an algorithm.

It's about pleasing your reader, too. If you don't know or understand an algorithm even is, it's just a detailed, step-by-step instruction set or formula for solving a problem or completing a task. It's a way of instructing the program, or platform, on how to do its job.

Fresh Content

The first thing Pinterest loves is fresh content. What defines fresh content? Pinterest now defines fresh content as:
- a new pin from your site (if it's just been published)
- a new pin with a new description

If you have a pin from last year, you can re-pin it from your site with a new description and it will be viewed as fresh content, and Tailwind would be a good place to put it on a Smart Loop. Your other option is a new pin of old content with a non-unique description. Fresh content can be created by simply changing the description.

The most notable thing that Pinterest has communicated to us bloggers is *you should always pin from your site and never re-pin from Pinterest.* Let your followers do the re-pinning for you.

What goes into high quality content

1. Create in-depth, lengthy posts. Think along the lines of the complete guide to X, where X is anything that is relevant to your brand rather than just posts that just skim the surface. Add screenshots, chapter, audio and/or research to support your post. Think outside the box. You don't have to just do text - you can add other things like graphics and video and audio and all sorts of media content that really helps your post to stand out. It also helps because people engage with content in different ways.

For me, personally, I enjoy reading posts, but other people I know love to watch videos and would rather watch a video than read a blog post. It really depends on your audience and the types of people that you are going after, so you want to make sure that you can mix it up so that you have different options for your audience.

2. Don't be afraid to do what others aren't. Sometimes I get questions from people who say there is nobody else in my niche who is doing this right now, should I do it or is it a bad idea? I usually tell them it kind of depends on the idea but almost always, I tell them that they should just go for it. They should try to do this thing where they are thinking outside the box and doing what other people aren't, because that is what is going to help you stand out.

Also, create evergreen content. Evergreen is a buzzword that basically means "timeless content", so it's not content where you are including a lot of dates or a lot of things that could be outdated in a month or something like that. It's content where somebody could read it a year from now and it will still be relevant. The content could be from the year 2013 and still be relevant if it's considered evergreen.

3. Add content upgrades to your post. We used to call these "upsells". Content upgrades are basically just additional pieces of content that somebody can get if they subscribe to get that piece of content from your post. You don't need to have a subscription model for content upgrades, but you could theoretically turn it into an email series. You could just give it away – but collect that email address – don't just have a download on your site without collecting information. For example, a content upgrade example would be like a free checklist. If your audience reads the post about some sort of step by step tutorial and then you could have this free PDF checklist that will help them in accomplishing the steps in your tutorial. You could give that away for free; that would be an awesome content upgrade. It's a different form of media that upgrades your blog post, or what I like to do is to say subscribe to get my freebie or my free content upgrade. They are subscribing because they really want this free thing that you created and you are growing your email list at the same time.

Content upgrades are a way to create more high-quality content. When people arrive on your site from Pinterest, you want them to be wowed, because people on Pinterest are clicking over to tons of different sites every day. So why would they click over to your site and then stick around? It's because you have a strong focus and very high-quality content. You want to have that high-quality content to keep those people around and not just those kind of passerby Pinterest users who are just looking at your content and collecting one little morsel from you. You want them to subscribe, buy your products and become forever fans.

Now if you only focus on getting new visitors and don't work on creating great content, then it's like opening up a bakery where all you sell are stale muffins. Yucky. Basically, if you create a great focus, you'll have a focus, sure, but you only focus on getting new visitors. You're opening this bakery, and people are coming into your bakery - all these new visitors, but then when they arrive into your bakery, they're like, "These are stale muffins! Sure, there are a lot of them but it's all stale!" So they leave and don't come back. You want to open up your bakery online that people love, where all the muffins are fresh and steamy hot, where it's really high quality, where maybe you even have some new muffin recipes for people to sample, and some things that people aren't doing with their content. You're standing out, you're being unique and you're really keeping those visitors and turning them into fans.

Step 1: high-quality content development

It all starts with a title. Titles are important because they are often what get people to click through. Once you enable rich pins, they'll also be prominently displayed below each of your pins. The title of your post is going to be displayed in bold text below your pin. So you want your title to be enticing and persuasive and interesting in order to get people to want to click it.

If you are creating great graphics, your title will be on your blog post image too. It's imperative that you have a strong title so that people are wanting to click through. But do not overthink it. In fact, you should be able to come up with a whole month's worth of titles and headlines in five minutes. Great titles are persuasive, realistic. They don't over embellish, so you don't want to tell people a lie in the title, you want to be realistic. They share value and they're SEO friendly (Search Engine Optimization friendly).

Basically, they include keywords or phrases that somebody would be searching for to find your post. Titles that tend to do well. So here are a few examples:

- List posts always do well; "10 Ways to Do Something", "Unique Ideas for Summer".
- "How to do", "how to" posts do well on Pinterest; "How I Created the Step by Step Guide to..."
- People love steps; step-by-step guides perform well and get shared dozens of times over.

Overall, lists and "how to" posts are very enticing especially on Pinterest.

Step 2 : high-quality images and design...

What kinds of images or photos will you use in your post? What brand story will you tell? If you take your own photos, aim to take them in bright, natural light. You can get great photos even with an iPhone if you're using natural light. Make sure that you have bright photos, crisp photos. You want your colors to stand out and you don't want to take them in a dark room because your photos are just not going to look as good.

Bright, natural light is really important, and then also telling your brand story, making sure that your imagery is consistent. Now if you use stock images, find images that compliment your brand. Don't use dark images if your brand is fun and upbeat. It's important to find stock images that also match your branding. Remember your photos convey your vibe, so make sure the imagery you choose is on brand. You want your photos to be on brand to really convey your vibe and that's also going to help you stand out on Pinterest and in the blogging world.

Some great sites for non-corporate looking stock images exist and they are some great resources for images that don't look so cheesy.

Here are a few of my favorites:

• Death to the Stock Photo. They have a free and a paid version.

• Bloguettes Stock that Rocks.

• Stocksy, they have a pay per photo plan. So do the other two, Death to the Stock and Bloguettes. They have a subscription model where you pay a monthly fee and you have access to all their photos. Stocksy is a little bit different, you pay per each photo but they have really nice, really high-quality photos.

• PicJumbo, they have free and paid photos.

• UnSplash, as far as I know, they only have free photos.

• KerrieLegend.com – I offer tech mockups and styled stock photos there.

All of these sites are awesome options for finding beautiful stock images. Many of them are free that you can use on your blog posts.

Tip time! Batch your own photos. Batching works in all facets of running a blog or business, but the idea is simple: do several days of work of the same task all at once. Take all your photos for the week all at once in like an hour. Set aside 1-2 hours a week and take all your photos for the week or month, just get it all out of the way and batch it together so you're not spending 15 minutes here to 45 minutes there, you're doing it all at once, getting it all out the way so you can just set up your equipment, get it all done and have all those photos finished. This is going to save you so much time. It also works great for writing content. If you're having trouble getting your content finished, then just set aside a couple hours a week and work on your content so that you can schedule it out and have it finished.

I teach a different course apart from Pinterest on how to maximize your social media strategy and enhance your productivity so you can get back to being more creative and producing more writing. Or, more time for family, which is always great! Check out my website at kerrielegend.com/courses to learn more about that course.

Step 3 : structure your content...

Honestly, you can be a mediocre writer and still make it as a blogger, (trust me I've seen plenty of them, even articles from great writers with mediocre blogs) primarily because many blogs don't only rely on writing. There are a lot of blogs out there like fashion, lifestyle, or food blogs where you don't necessarily need to be a great writer. Of course, it will help, but if that's not your strongpoint then you could still make it with beautiful photos and other components of your blog.

But, no matter what you do, your writing needs structure. People nowadays will look at huge paragraphs of writing of text and simply say "ugh". It's just. Too. Much. They can't process that amount of information. They're not going to read a huge paragraph of text. You need structure. Great structuring includes short paragraphs; try to keep them to five lines or less. You don't want to have this huge mass of text. Five lines or less is what you are aiming for, short paragraphs.

Use headings to divide each section, so that it's easier to scan your content and find exactly what the article is about and if they want to read it. Lists are a great way to divide up content too. Consider using headings in conjunction with lists. So, you can have point 1, 2, 3, etc. and create a great-looking, structured post.

Step 4 : create clear paths...

When someone arrives on your site, what do you want them to do? Make it obvious. Most people honestly don't do this and this is a huge thing for any type of website. You want to have a clear path. What do you want people to do when they arrive on your site? On my own site, I have a "Start Here" area. It helps foster sign-ups to my email list. What do you want them to do when they arrive from Pinterest on a specific post? What's the end goal? Is it just to have them read your post? Is it to have them subscribe to your Instagram account or your email list? Is it to have them purchase your e-book?

Think about what's the end goal of them arriving on your site and then make it obvious. You shouldn't set up your posts so that they read one and then spend five minutes figuring out where everything else is. You want it to be obvious what you want them to do.

Examples of some clear paths that you can implement on your blog:

• Add categories to your menu bar at the top. Categories with the most relevant topic to your blog that make it easy for people to view the other content in a specific category that they might be interested in.

• Include email opt-in forms in your header, below your posts and in your side bar. Add a bunch of email opt-in forms so that in case your reader doesn't see the first one, like in your header or below your posts. They might see another one like in your side bar or maybe you even have a pop up, so include multiple opt-in forms.

• Include related posts below your post to keep them browsing, clicking around, getting more engaged and interested in your website.

• Add social media icons below posts and encourage them to follow you.

• Include images of your products or services in your sidebar, letting them know how they can work with you.

These are just some examples of different clear paths that you can implement on your website to make it more obvious what you want somebody to do once they get on your site.

Speaking of clear paths, I want to share a clear path that I use on my own website. When someone visits my website, this is the very first thing that they see, and you can see the "Start Here" button on my menu. I get them introduced to my content and grab a sign-up. I also have a pop-up that says "I'd love to send you my resource library and give you updates!"

This is the path that I want people to take when they visit my website; sign up and get on my email list. I have different opt-in forms around my website. This one is the most prominent and the one everyone sees when they come to my site for the first time. I recommend brainstorming and really thinking about what that clear path is for you. For me, it's my email list, and just a little spoiler alert, it's what I recommend for you as well.

I think you should really focus on your email list, but maybe you have another path that you want to take. You just need to be intentional about what that clear path is that you want people to go on when they visit your website and then make your website geared towards having people do or take that one specific action.

This is not about cluttering your website with tons of options, side bar graphics, flashing banners and confusion. This is about zeroing in on what is that one intentional message and purpose of your website and how are you going to get people to take action in the direction of that message. Sometimes we forget all about that and assume our readers know what we do. Trust me, they don't know. Tell them. Make it clear.

Step 5 : what is the takeaway ?

For every single post you write, you should be able to answer specifically what is somebody going to get out of reading this post? What's the takeaway? Posts with a strong takeaway or value are ones that get re-pinned and increase your followers and fans. People are not going to re-pin your posts, or click through to your posts if it is vague or hard to understand what the value of the post is. You need to make it extremely obvious what the value is, and define what's the takeaway.

What are they going to get out of reading your post? A takeaway can be that you taught them something. Maybe it's a tutorial, a "how to" post, etc. - any type of post where you are teaching them how to do something. It could also be that you inspired or encouraged them in some way. It doesn't have to be quite as tangible; maybe it's more of self development or an encouragement type of post. The takeaway can be a little bit less tangible in that sense, but you still want to be able to very specifically answer, what is someone going to get out of reading this post?

Step 6 : Give, give and give some more (plan on giving, for like, forever)

So many bloggers nowadays operate under the idea that you can publish blog posts that are short and don't go into too many details. It seems like a lot of bloggers are more under the mentality that they want to publish posts often, but it doesn't really matter if they're super, super high quality, but that's kind of backward thinking in my opinion. That is just not a solid model for your blog and it's not going to create raving fans.

If you're just giving them a few details, you're not really giving them the whole story, and then it's not going to create these huge raving fans that love, love, love your website. Instead, give as much as possible. Don't write posts that barely scratch the surface on a topic. I'll say that again. Don't write posts that barely scratch the surface on a topic. Write posts that answer just about every question someone might have on a specific topic. You want to be detailed, you want to give the goods.

Think of it this way, write content worth selling. Write content that you could probably sell and make money from and then just give it away for free. You want to give, give, give so that when you do eventually want to sell something or you try to grow your audience, then your audience is already super engaged in what you're doing because you've given them so much awesome content already.

Again, don't be afraid to think differently. It is all good if you want to try something a little over the top. People are used to what they see in blog posts so shaking things up will help you standout. Try adding video, audio, or anything else that will level up your post. It's so, so, so okay if you haven't seen others in your niche do what you want to do. It's a good thing because you really want to stand out and it's hard to stand out if all you're doing are the same things that you see other people doing. So really try to think a little bit over the top, think a little bit differently, elaborate on what other people are doing and remind yourself that it's okay to be a little bit different.

JUST TO RECAP...

• Killer content includes a click worthy, descriptive title, great imagery and brand imagery.

• An easy-to-read structure-so remember we have our short paragraphs divided with easy to find and scan headings.

• A clear path of action, so ask yourself "what do you want somebody to do after they read this post?"

• An obvious takeaway, so ask yourself "what are they going to get out of the post?"

• Content that doesn't just brush the surface. Content that goes into detail, that gives them more facts, more information, that answers their questions before they ask them.

If you do all these things for every single post your blog is going to grow like a weed: uber fast in a good way (some weeds, like dandelions, are awesomely sweet). Killer content is the foundation of what you do with your blog. Then, once you create that killer content, and then on top of having a focus and a defined tribe, you'll get on Pinterest in the next chapters, and you're just going to blossom. It's going to grow really fast and your brand is going to grow and just be a lot more clearly defined and loved by your people. I'm very excited to get into the next chapters to show you some more.

4 PINTEREST PROFILE

The median age of a Pinterest user is 40, however, the majority of active pinners are below 40.

In this chapter, we're going to be talking about mastering your Pinterest Profile because everyone wants to make a good first impression, right? That first impression is going to often dictate whether or not someone follows you and shares your pins.

Whenever you are using Pinterest, or really whenever you're using your blog or business in general, you should be asking yourself... "who am I attracting, or who am I trying to attract?" The point of it is that this is not about you; we're creating your entire brand, your entire blog or business for your tribe. This is not about you or your personal preferences or your interests or your hobbies; we're not using Pinterest for any of that. Don't be sad about that! Focusing on who you're trying to attract is going to bring you much bigger growth.

Step 1: become a business account

Step 1 in creating a explosive Pinterest profile is to become a business account. A business account gives you access to Pinterest Analytics. We'll be talking about that later in a future chapter. If you want to switch to a business account, which I highly recommend even if you're not a business, is go to business.pinterest.com to switch to a business account.

Once you're established as a business account, you can also use the Pinterest Verify plugin for WordPress to upload a special code that they're going to give you on to your website. This makes it extra easy. Now if you have something else like Squarespace, no problem, you won't be able to use that specific plugin but you can still upload the code that they give you in to become a business account.

If you can't figure this out yourself, then just email Pinterest Support, and I've heard around the block that they will help you out. So why become a business account? Well, because you get access to some really cool features like analytics, promoted pins and rich pins. It's really in your best interest to become a business account even if you're not selling anything.

Step 2 : apply for rich pins

Rich pins add your website name and your blog post title to every single pin from your website. This creates awesome brand recognition where people see your blog pot title or your content title. They see your brand or blog name right below the pin and it just creates that kind of recognition where they see it in their feed and they start to recognize your name or your blog post title. You definitely want to get rich pins after you apply and get approved for a business account. This is just going to amplify your Pinterest account and help you start to rank higher in the Pinterest feed. It's totally worth it.

Step 3: create a killer profile

Your profile should tell people what you do or how you help people, who exactly you serve. It should include a call to action to join your email list and you should include a photo or a logo. I know this is kind of a controversy so let me kind of break it down for you.

I believe that more often than not, you should be using a photo of your friendly old looking face. I want to see your pretty face. I want to be able to connect to a real human when I go to your Pinterest profile. You can use a logo if you are a bigger corporation, but unless you have a ton of employees and the business is really not about you at all, then you could use a logo. For most things like handmade businesses, blogs and businesses that don't have too many employees and really feature you as the owner, for example on your about page, I recommend using a photo instead. And lastly, you want to include keywords in your name.

Let's talk about the bio formula. I let you know that you want to include a few sentences in your actual bio on Pinterest and this is the formula I recommend using. You can start with "I help" or "I inspire", "I teach" – whatever kind of verb you want to use there. And then who do you help, so I help entrepreneurs, I help busy moms, I help lawyers – whoever you help.

Do, become or learn, then what do you help them do, become or learn. So I help law students become lawyers. Basically, you're just showing people the kind of progression that you help them with. I help people who have no sense of style become fashionistas, so you can kind of see that progression there.

And then lastly, you want to include a call to action, like "Sign Up for My Free Seven Day Course" or "My Free Cheat Sheet". Give them some sort of incentive to sign up for your email list and then include a link where they can sign up. You can see this all in action on my own profile at pinterest.com/kerrielegend.

JUST TO RECAP...

Making an awesome first impression on Pinterest.

First you want to get a business account and rich pins, yes even if you're not a business.

- You want to write a bio that tells people how you help them.
- You should use a photo usually, but sometimes a logo.
- You want to have a call to action in your bio and you want to have keywords in your profile name because then it makes your profile searchable.

5 CREATING BOARDS

Half of Pinterest users earn $50K or greater per year, with 10 percent of Pinterest-ing households making greater than $125K.

A lrighty, now this is a big topic – creating boards. Think of your boards like categories on a blog. If you have a blog, then maybe you have different categories for the types of topics that you discuss on your blog. Think of your boards on Pinterest as your categories. This is basically asking the question, "what is your brand all about?" You're going to come up with some topics that your brand is all about and then morph those into your boards on Pinterest.

Conduct a board cleanse

Strategy is the name of the game here when it comes to board cleansing. Don't freak out - what I mean by that is delete or make secret any boards that aren't relevant to your target audience. Delete pins that are not evergreen or do not have relevance technology or application-wise anymore. You may have a Pinterest account already which is totally fine, but you might have some boards on your account that just aren't going to be relevant to that ideal audience that you're trying to attract. What I'm saying is either delete those boards or just turn them into secret boards so no one sees them.

Then once you do that, add any new boards that attract your target audience, and I'd aim for at least 15 to 20 boards in total. I have around 16-18. Of course, you can have more than that, but at the bare minimum, aim for 15 to 20. Now when I say that you want boards that attract your target audience, I'm saying think about those categories that you might put on your blog that would attract the right people to your website and then turn those categories into boards on Pinterest. So really, just think of the different general categories and topics that your target audience would be searching for and then create a board out of them.

Move your pins around

If you want to move your pins when you are cleaning up your boards, maybe you have a board that has a few pins that are good and another board that has another few pins that are good and you just want to combine them into one board, you can move 50 pins at a time. If you go to one of your boards, you'll see this kind of four arrow symbol at the top. If you click that symbol then this second image will pop where it says "move", and then you can click the move button and then just click on any pin that you want to move to another board. This can make it much easier to clean up your pins because you can move up to 50 pins at one time.

Add targeted boards

If you're having trouble coming up with new boards, maybe you've got 10 great board ideas but you don't really have any ideas for 5 to 10 more boards to add to your account, here is a little tip for you. On

Pinterest, go into the little search bar at the top, type in some of your main keywords or things that your brand or business or blog are about, or the type of things that your target audience would be searching for, or any categories you already have. Type any of those things into Pinterest search field and then this cool thing will pop up.

You can see there is this row of all of these other keywords that someone might be searching for. Basically, Pinterest is giving you some ideas of different things that you could search for based on that keyword that you typed into the search field. So I searched "calligraphy", maybe you are a hand lettering blogger or maybe you are a calligrapher or something along those lines. I type that in there and then you see all of these different ideas and you can also toggle the arrows on the left or right side for even more ideas.

Based on this feedback, I could create another board called Calligraphy Quotes or Calligraphy Alphabet. So I'm coming up with new ideas based on that one little seedling of an idea that I had before. If you're struggling to come up with multiple boards for your Pinterest profile, try this tip; I think you'll really enjoy it.

Now overall, your boards should only target topics that your ideal reader or customer would be searching for. So again, we're not creating personal boards, we're only creating things that our target audience would be searching for, and it should be within the realm of your niche. For example, maybe you target women who want to eat a healthy diet. So women who want to eat a healthy diet may also be interested in makeup, that might be something that some of them are interested in, but I wouldn't create a board called Makeup or Beauty because that's not really relevant to eating healthy. You see what I mean? So don't look for those loop holes where you kind of could add a board that maybe they would be interested in. You really want to keep it within the realm of your niche and that attracts the audience you want to serve.

Use straightforward board names

Now for your board titles, use words that are straightforward, not flowery or poetic. I know that sometimes we have a tendency on Pinterest to create board titles that sound really unique because Pinterest is visual, it's creative, but it's also a search engine. You need to be straightforward with your naming conventions because otherwise your boards are not going to be searchable.

Think about the words that someone would be typing into Pinterest to search for something and then name your board that particular keyword or topic. Don't go too crazy here, just be as straightforward as you can. I know it might sound a little bit bland, but they're going to fall in love with your content and that's where the flowers and poetry live. It doesn't live in your keywords; it lives in the actual content that you are creating.

Fill up the boards

Now it's time to fill your boards up with relevant content. I like to search for one topic at a time, so I just go up to the search field on Pinterest, type in a topic for that particular board and I go on a pinning spree. I just pin 50 or 100 things at one time if I'm starting a new board and I just fill it up with a lot of great content. So that way, I don't have to gradually fill it up over several months, I can just do it in one fell swoop.

Stay tuned for the Tailwind tutorials in a future chapter because I'm going to be showing you how to schedule pins, so if you do go on a pinning spree like this, instead of pinning them all publicly at once, you can actually pin them so that they stagger and then go out over the span of a week or two.

Now a pro tip: if you're only following people who pin things that are relevant to your target audience, then your feed will have tons of content that you can quickly pin. So in this case, if you want to be a really fast pinner who wants to save a ton of time on Pinterest, I highly recommend unfollowing people who pin things that you personally like, but aren't relevant to your niche or your target audience, and then start to follow people in your niche who pin things that your target audience would like.

The reason for that is when you log into Pinterest, your Pinterest newsfeed with all those pins that you see, will only have content that you can pin to your brand's Pinterest account. That makes it very easy to find new content because every time you log in, you're going to be seeing a lot of new content from people in your niche or people that pin things that are relevant to the people you are trying to attract.

So you could just re-pin that content quickly and be done. Now I know some of you love using Pinterest and I don't blame you, it's a pretty awesome tool for personal use too, so if you want to keep following people that you love for your own personal use, you can absolutely do that too, just know that it might take you a little bit longer to find new stuff to pin to your boards or you could just create a new account solely for your personal use.

JUST TO RECAP...

• Do a board cleanse to clean up your account.

• Include at least 15 to 20 targeted boards.

• Use straightforward board titles, no poetry or flowery language.

• Fill up your boards, so we're aiming to have at least 15 to 100 pins on every single board on your account.

I know that this is a big undertaking so if you can't do it right away, no problem. You have several weeks to be able to fit this into your schedule, but once you start doing this you'll start seeing your followers increase.

6 PINTEREST CLEANUP

30% of all US social media users are Pinterest users.

First Things First - Clean Up Your Profile

Does your Pinterest profile match your branding? Does your Pinterest profile match your website with colors, fonts, and content? Do your keywords reflect the content you write about, are there descriptions in each board, pin, and in your profile? Each of these areas - boards, pins, profile description - should have a lot of relevant and unique phrased keywords, and should also clearly show and illustrate what you are all about.

Individual Board Assessment and Optimization

Pinterest boards communicate your overall message with regards to content. From a first glance, visitors should be able to understand easily what you do for a living, what you're all about, and what you're interested in. Make sure that you have a board that contains all of your own domain pins in it, so that people can dig into that board and start reading what you've written. They like to test you out, take your blog for a spin... before they necessarily follow you. Make sure your domain board is listed first in your Pinterest account.

Re-evaluate Your Keywords – How you name your boards matters in terms of keywords. Searches on Pinterest are reliant on the naming conventions of your boards, so be sure that you keep your board names straightforward and conventional. Don't do anything fancy that would mess up search. If your boards aren't performing well, then re-evaluate your keywords and board title. Move them to a secret status if you're just using them for your own benefit, as they may not serve a purpose for your followers.

Deleting Pins – You don't necessarily need to delete pins unless you're approaching the account limit of 300k. What happens if you sell, for example, a limited item and your inventory is dwindled to nothing? What I would do is redirect on your site to something else to let the visitor know the item is no longer available but you have other things for sale. Just find a similar item so that you don't have to delete your pin, which is probably on several boards already on other accounts.

Board Sections – Board sections are more of a user tool currently on Pinterest, and haven't been factored into the algorithm to date, to my knowledge. Sectioning can help keep things organized, but you may want to opt for creating a new board for something rather than creating sections for search engine purposes.

How often should you do a board cleanup? I do it once every quarter. I take a look at, evaluate low-performing pins, move some to secret if they still serve a purpose for me, but then get rid of things that are redundant or no longer relevant. (Technology changes is a great reason to do this.) It really depends on how many people you have looking at your profile. I have 100 new followers a day, so this is something that is very important for me to do. Only add boards when you feel like your business is either shifting into a new line or you're adding content that simply doesn't fit into the boards you currently have.

How Effective Are Group Boards?

The whole point of group boards was to collaborate. But to date, group boards have become dumping grounds for pins without active re-pinning. Only join group boards that are active, have a lot of engagement, and have members actively re-pinning. You can easily check their effectiveness using Tailwind or another Pinterest-approved software program.

If you're part of a group board that isn't a good target market for your audience, like a free-for-all type group board, leave the board and focus more on your personal boards, because that's where you'll have more success in growth. Never put more focus on group boards than you do on your own boards. People make the mistake of thinking that group boards are the fast ticket to gaining popularity and viral status, but actually, focusing on your own boards with descriptions, keywords, and such are much more important.

Create a Specific Board Order

Keep your own domain board at the top, with the next five being your most popular boards, and then your less-related boards, and group boards at the bottom. You'll want to keep the boards that have the most engagement at the top because they speak the most about your brand. Let your own boards shine first. Group boards are only secondary afterthoughts.

For board covers, keep the colors and images related to your brand, and be consistent with your font use. I insist on putting board cover titles on mine because sometimes the eyes drift to the visual and not necessarily the board name at the top as a header. Spend some quality time working your board covers - having an impressive first impression could mean the difference of getting a new follower or not.

Pinterest says, "We distribute your content to your followers first to figure out what is resonating. From there, we distribute your best-performing pins to other people who are looking for ideas like yours." Therefore, you want engaged followers, not just any follower. While follower growth isn't the primary mission, it does help with reach and having more and more people find you.

What I discovered in December 2018 to January 2019 was that my follower count was starting to mushroom as my account climbed to 10 million + monthly followers. An average day was becoming around 130-165 new followers a day. So just know that as you grow, and as your reach starts to expand, things will start to mushroom for you, as well.

Google's Accelerated Mobile Pages Update

Google recently released a new update which prioritizes accelerated mobile pages. Accelerated Mobile Pages Project (AMP) is a website publishing technology developed by Google as a competitor to Facebook's Instant Articles. As users of Pinterest, we knew this was coming with the emergence of mobile app use on the rise. And what this meant for Pinterest, was that instead of competing against Pinterest pins for ranking in the Google search feed, now *your posts* (not just your pins) have a greater opportunity of being seen.

Image Size

763x1102 is the Pinterest-approved size, and what most WYSIWYG image apps like Canva, PicMonkey, and Easel use, but most everyone tends to use a 600 x 900 guideline for image size. You have a limited area of space to show your content, including a pin title, sub-header, image, and perhaps even a screenshot of an opt-in freebie. So make sure you get everything you can on it (without crowding the image) that you feel is most relevant and must-see.

You're All Set

Now that your boards are clean, ready, organized, formatted, have proper keywords and titles, as well as descriptions, you're ready to start pinning. Last pointer before you go full throttle with pinning from your domain - use 5 template designs for your pinning. The goal here is to make sure that your pins are recognizable and memorable - so be consistent with your pin design, and you'll have great success.

7 PINTEREST BRANDING STRATEGY

50% of Pinterest users are from the US.

A lright everybody, welcome back. In this chapter, we're talking about building a brand on Pinterest and really getting the juice out of that brand recognition.

Does it matter what you pin ?...

Yes. It does matter what you pin, because you don't just want to pin a bunch of random stuff. You should be pinning high-quality on-brand content.

That's the key here; on-brand content. Remember, you are pinning for your audience, not yourself. So in this book, I'm not showing you how to create a beautiful, personal Pinterest with all of your random things that you are interested in. We are creating a Pinterest profile for a brand whether that brand is your blog, your business – whatever it may be, but we are creating this Pinterest for your audience.

Now, you can still pin a lot of stuff that's interesting to you, but again, we're pinning for your audience, not for you. Let's get into it.

Building a strong brand...

A strong brand will help you stand out because it breeds consistency. People are going to start to recognize you and your work. Strong branding can consist of a lot of different things.

Your branding will be consistent if you stick to 3 to 5 complementary colors that you use on everything, not necessarily all at once. But you want to stick to these 3 to 5 complementary colors so that your branding looks very consistent and starts to stand out to people in their feed.

If they consistently see the same images or same style of images over and over again even though they are for a different post, people are going to start to take notice and get curious about those posts. So you want to stick to 3 to 5 complementary colors, and this works for everything in terms of your brand, not just on Pinterest, but definitely for your Pinterest images as well. And of course, you have the Pinterest handout for this book to help you discover some solid branding points.

Also, stick to two to three fonts only and always. I usually like to pick a font for headings, like headings, big fonts that you want to use, then subheadings, any font that you'll use for a sub-heading and then the text, text font. So 2 to 3 fonts only, sometimes your heading and subheading font will be the same and you only have two fonts.

Avoid succumbing to the shiny object syndrome where you see a pretty font and decide to use it even though it has nothing to do with your branding. You've got to be consistent with your brand.

Your branding is consistent if you have a particular vibe or value to share, so not only do you know who you are but you know who you're not. I know that my brand is not like in your face punk rock, like cussing. I know that there's other brands out there that are more like that where they appeal to a different type of audience, but that's not my brand. It's important not only to know who your brand is but also who your brand is not.

Your brand is confusing if you see a new color, palette or new font and you just want to try it. That's okay in the beginning when you're testing out a lot of different things, maybe you're a new blogger, and honestly I think it is okay if you are brand-new because you can't really find what you love until you test out a lot of different things. But once you hit, let's say the six-month point, you should really create a more solid and consistent brand.

If you change your website's design or branding every month, you will confuse your audience. Now if this is a problem for you, if you really enjoy design, you really like switching up your blog design all the time, then hire someone to do it for you. You are much less likely to constantly renovate a brand that someone else created for you and that you paid for. Hire me to do your design – it's not overly expensive but it bites you just enough in the wallet while making you look amazing online all the while zapping your desire to change what I create for you.

Your brand is also confusing if you don't have a particular voice. Honestly, finding your voice with your brand just means that you found the confidence to write as yourself, that's it. I think a lot of people get confused about how to find their blogging voice, but really your voice is just talking as yourself, at your core.

Remember, create your brand around your tribe, not yourself. So create your branding around your tribe, not yourself. Again, this book about creating a popular blog and business, is not about creating something for you, we're throwing ourselves off the boat entirely. We are creating all of this stuff for our audience, our tribe.

Step 1: decide what you are an authority on…

Now this is going to be harder – if you want to grow your Pinterest profile, it is going to be harder to grow if you pin all the things. The same goes for your blog, your website, and your business. If you don't have that focus that you are the authority or the leader on something in particular, it's going to be a lot harder to grow. Just like with your blog, your Pinterest profile needs a focus, the same focus as your blog obviously, because you want to appeal to the same audience.

You can become an expert and authority in a certain niche. You want to become an expert and an authority in a certain niche, not just spreading yourself too thin and touching surface on 10 topics, but picking one topic that you are a leader in. And the content you pin should fall into this niche. Again, everything is very consistent, your brand is obvious and on point. Of course, asking yourself the questions, who are you pinning for, who is your tribe, who is your audience, and deciding who that person is, what you can pin for them and become a leader for that person, will drive your blog and Pinterest profile that much further.

Can you pin other stuff? If you are pinning for your tribe, can you pin stuff that isn't totally irrelevant to that first topic? It is important to become an authority on a certain topic, this is what is going to help you stand out, but you can still pin other things occasionally, just make sure that they are on brand for your audience. I share a lot of blogging tips, entrepreneur tips, social media tips, so honestly, I do not ever pin a recipe. I just don't. It's not part of my brand model at the moment, and may never be.

Everything should still tie together for that ideal audience member, should still be very cohesive to your brand. But if they are too off brand or too random, then create secret boards so you can see them but others can't, so if there is just a recipe that you are dying to make then just pin it to a secret board. Don't worry, you can still use Pinterest to its full potential. You don't need to just throw everything away, but just create secret boards to keep those things for yourself that you don't want your audience to see.

Step 2: create a consistent aesthetic...

You'll probably see that on my own kerrielegend.com board that my pins all kind of look the same, don't they? When people see my pins in their feed, they immediately recognize them as something they've either seen before or if they've been to my website, then they know that it is my pin. All my pins are branded in some way.

Now, you want to create your own visually consistent pins for that same reason, to build brand recognition. If your blog is full of color, joy and happiness, then you want to create images that are colorful and happy too, because again, it gives you that brand consistency. If you create products that have a certain aesthetic to them, you want to pin images that have that aesthetic quality to them as well, because again, you are creating a brand on Pinterest and people aren't just going to follow you for your content, they're going to follow you for everything else that you are pinning too, so you really need to think of your pinning strategy in this kind of holistic sense. Think of it this way, you want people to associate you with a certain aesthetic.

JUST TO RECAP...

• Decide which topics are at the core of your brand, what are you going to be pinning about, and who are you trying to attract. You should be answering those questions every time you pin something to your account.

• Decide on your aesthetic style, so what kind of pins are you going to be sharing, do you have some sort of style that you're going to stick to, is that important to your audience.

8 DESIGNING THE PERFECT PIN

Pinterest is on its way to make $700 million in revenue this year.

Whether you consider yourself a designer or not, I'm going to show you how to design share-worthy pins, so the things that go into great pins, and a simple strategy for creating beautiful pins even if you've never touched a piece of design software. Are you ready for this? Let's do it.

The perfect pin checklist

The perfect pin checklist includes:

1. It should be vertical – I recommend roughly 800 x 1200 pixels. You can kind of skew this a little bit, but the general concept is you want your pin to be tall rather than wide and horizontal. The reason for this is because vertical pins just appear larger in the Pinterest feed. You want your pins to appear larger because then they are more

likely to be seen, which means they are more likely to get re-pins and click throughs to your website.

The first thing that did change in the algorithm and that you need to be paying attention to is image size. Images need to be a 2:3 ratio or they will not be distributed. My preferred image sizes are 600 x 900 or 735 x 1102. You can do up to 1260 in length but they won't be shown often, especially on mobile. All images you create moving forward need to match up with these sizes but you don't need to spend the time to going back and updating all your old images.

2. Use on brand colors and fonts – we've talked about brand consistency before and it is so important. When I started my blog, I fell in love with a new font pretty much every week – it's hard as a designer to stick with a brand and now show off all your millions of fonts (believe me – so hard!). All of my Pinterest images and blog post images looked completely different week after week. As a graphic designer, it's SOOOO tempting to try out new fonts and use them everywhere. Trust me – it's practically unbearable. But for consistency, I have to stick with the fonts that I have chosen. Eventually, I realized that people were not able to recognize my blog. I was dazzling them with color and fonts and layouts galore. It was like every time you met up with a friend and then they change everything about their appearance and you are like, "Wait, I thought you looked different last week." This is how people are feeling about your website and your branding if you're constantly changing your hairstyle online, if you know what I mean. The solution to that is choosing a few fonts and a few colors and sticking with those throughout everything that you create for your brand.

3. Include large easy to read text – use a bit of text along with a great image. Including some text on your image to let people know what they're going to get out of clicking through to your post or product.

4. Include your website link –I've seen people who put a giant logo on their pin or they put their website link super huge somewhere on their pin, which I understand, you are excited about your blog or

your business. It totally makes sense and I'm sure I did the same thing too, but the fact of the matter is that people on Pinterest don't yet care about you, and I say that very lovingly, but you have to get people to care about you by getting them over to your website and seeing how awesome your products or your blog posts are, but for the time being, they don't really care too much about you or your logo or your website name. For now, it's just there to kind of build that brand recognition in a small way and to kind of copyright your images to make sure that no one rips them off of Facebook. We want to use that website link in case your pin ends up somewhere else in the Internet universe, but we don't want it to be the focal point. We really want your headline to be the focal point of your pin.

5. Include a screenshot of your incentive – If you are using opt-in incentives or content upgrades which we're going to be talking about more in a later section, then I highly recommend including a little screenshot of your incentive on your pin itself and then something that lets people know what they're going to get for free. I don't just say free workbook without a screenshot because I feel that when people see the actual workbook, they are more likely to want it because they can visualize it on their computer or in their hands, because they can actually see what it looks like. It's more powerful to have an image of that freebie that they're going to get and you can just put that right on top of your Pinterest image.

6. Save your files using keywords – Now you can't really see this one inside of this image here, but when you are saving your image onto your computer and then uploading it to your website, you want to use some keywords in the file name. If you're just uploading something from your camera, then it might sound something like CYX_542.jpeg which is not really searchable unless you're searching for something called CYX_542, which is probably not the case. So in this case, every time you create a blog post, title your image that you're going to pin on to Pinterest with a keyword. Whatever the topic of your blog post is, or whatever kind of product you are going to be pinning, make sure that you save it as something that's relevant.

I might save it as something like blogging-tips. If you are creating a meal plan, you might save it as paleomealplan.jpeg. You just want to name it with some keywords in the file name so that your image is a little bit more searchable.

7. Use evergreen content – the best content on Pinterest is evergreen content. I'm going to explain a little bit more about that in just a second, but keep that word, evergreen, in your mind for now. Now all the pins on Pinterest have the same width so you can imagine a horizontal pin with the same width as a vertical pin, it's just going to look a lot smaller. That's why you want to use vertical pins. Now, back to evergreen content, which I briefed you on in a past chapter. Of course you want to use evergreen content. Evergreen content is essentially just content that is timeless. It's as useful today as it will be in one year, so it is not time sensitive like a pin for an event or a webinar or something along those lines. Think of timeless evergreen content that you can create and then pin that on to Pinterest.

Now Pro tip: if you are new, maybe you don't have a lot of content yet, maybe you are a new business owner, a new blogger and you just don't have a lot of things to pin yet. If that's the case, what I recommend doing is creating multiple pin templates for each blog post or each product that you have and then pin them all.

So instead of just creating one template for that blog post, you can create three templates, so now if you have 10 blog posts and each one has three different images that are great for Pinterest inside of it, then that's essentially 30 things that you can pin on to Pinterest even though you only have 10 blog posts or 10 products. This is also a good way to A/B test your pins or your headlines. You can create similar templates.

Now, here's a disclosure. I have over 100+ templates just for Pinterest that I can use, and I make them available on my website for purchase if you want them (they're amazing.) You want to again, stay on brand with the same fonts and colors, but maybe just change the layout or something or change the text or the headline and then test it. Layout changes are perfectly acceptable within your brand.

You're not violating any image rules there. You can try different wording or different phrasing or different layout for your pin and then see which one gets more re-pins, and then you'll have a good idea of which one you should continue using in the future.

More design tips

If you're not a designer, maybe you are struggling to create on-brand pin templates or any kind of designs for your website, so try this easy pin design. Put a transparent layer on top of a photo, so you can do this very easily in Photoshop (you can get a month of it for FREE).

You basically just put a slab of color on top of a photo and then just fiddle with the opacity a little bit so that it's not a completely opaque image but you can see the photo behind it. Then just add some text on top of that and voila! You have created a stellar Pinterest image.

Of course, you may want to add some other things that we talked about earlier like your website name down at the bottom, but in general, you can create something that looks like this and it looks great, it will work extraordinarily well on Pinterest. It doesn't have to be super crazily designed. You don't have to do anything too complex. Although, beautifully, well-thought-out pins using unique layouts perform even better. Be sure to check them out on my website and change up your game to a whole new level.

You can create beautiful images in a really simple way. Again, just put that transparent layer on top, and you might want to use a color that goes with your branding and then just pop some text on top and you're good to go. For some design program recommendations, I recommend Photoshop for beginners. They have a free plan available. They also have a paid plan. I do not recommend apps like Canva because all the "good" images you have to pay for, and when you're on a budget, it's very tempting to "settle" for second best. The point is to impress people – so unless you're willing to spend $1+ per image, I would recommend other options. For people who want to get more design experience or who already have some design experience, I still recommend Photoshop. Photoshop is around $19 a month, so not too bad there.

JUST TO RECAP...

• Create pins that follow the rules of perfect pins that we went over.

• Create multiple pin images for each post if you don't have a lot of content yet.

9 THE PINTEREST SMART FEED

Pinterest is currently valued at more than $11 billion and aiming for an IPO in 2019 with $13-$15 billion valuations.

This chapter we're going to discuss how to master the Smart Feed on Pinterest and also what the heck the Smart Feed is. If you really want to get awesome results on Pinterest then this section is for you.

The Pinterest Smart Feed

It was introduced in late 2014 so it hasn't been around for a super long time. Pinterest used to display pins as newest first, now it displays them as best first, very much like a search engine would. You might have been worried that you could pin too many things and bother your followers, because if you're pinning 30 things at once, then when it displayed your pins as newest first, then all 30 pins would be displayed all at once. Now because of the Smart Feed, it displays them as best first. It basically ranks all of the pins that people share. If your pins are not best first, then you know what happens? They are not getting seen.

It judges each user with an internal ranking system to determine whose pins are the best. Bottom line, if Pinterest does not rank you highly, your pins won't be seen right away and sometimes not at all, so that kind of sucks if your pins are not getting seen by your followers. The Smart Feed has totally changed the game, but I am confident that I have cracked the code and I'm about to share it with you.

I just want to reiterate the fact that Pinterest is a search engine. So if you think about Google, Google has algorithms, really sophisticated algorithms where it is scanning all of the information out there to find the very best articles to rank first in its search engine. When you type in "taco recipe" on Google, it's finding you the best taco recipes, and it takes a lot of factors into consideration like who the site is, whether there are pictures, videos, how long the post is. There are a lot of different factors that go into Google's ranking system.

Now Pinterest has started implementing a similar ranking system where they don't want their users to just pull up random things that aren't very relevant or aren't very useful. They want people who use Pinterest to love Pinterest, so they internally created what is referred to as "user voice", which is part of their algorithm.

There are users who are not going to love Pinterest; they are casual users who are just looking for things to read and pin. They're not going to love Pinterest if every time they click through to an article, it's not very good, so that's why Pinterest has implemented this best first algorithm, much like a search engine like Google would. They are displaying pins as best first.

Now, if you remember only one thing from this book, remember this. Pinterest is a search engine not a social media platform. So like Google, it has an algorithm that ranks content from best and most relevant to its users, to irrelevant or weak content. If you're not incorporating SEO or search engine functionality onto your Pinterest account and with your pins and boards etc., then your pins are not going to be showing up at the top of people's feeds. They're going to be shoved at the bottom or maybe just not even seen. Ever.

Following the steps to outsmart the Smart Feed gives you the best shot at showing up at the top of people's feeds. The cornerstone of search engines is keywords, so we're going to be talking about keywords and how to implement them into your Pinterest account so that you can again the best results possible on Pinterest by using it as a search engine, not a social media platform.

A few Smart Feed factors

It's all about high-quality content. Everything in the Smart Feed revolves around high-quality content. That's basically the key to getting your content to rank higher. There are a few things that go into that as well.

Pins with more re-pins are assumed to be better. Pinterest isn't exactly reading all the articles out there. That would take forever. They are not ranking them hand by hand, one by one, but they look at a few different factors to see which pins appear to be the best. Pins with more re-pins are assumed to be better, and more high-quality, because it shows that people like those pins. Pins with descriptions are more easily found and shared.

So again, Pinterest is a search engine, so if you don't have a description on your pin, people are not going to be finding it as easily. If they can't find it, they can't re-pin it. Pinners who share consistently are ranked higher. People who are constantly pinning on Pinterest are assumed by Pinterest to be more high-quality pinners because they are in it to win it. Pins that lead to relevant links are better. Pinterest doesn't want its users to be clicking a bunch of links and have it lead to random websites or suspicious websites or broken links. They want it to lead to relevant links that the actual article that it says it's linking to. Relevant links are better.

Mastering the Smart Feed

Now let's master this smart feed, step-by-step. There are a few different ways, that we can go through it. Make sure that your pins are being seen in the Smart Feed and this will grow your account as well. If you are not doing these things, then I've got to tell you that your account is probably demoted in Pinterest's internal ranking system which is why it might be harder for your account to grow, why you might not be seeing as many re-pins on your pins or on your account. So factoring in the Smart Feed algorithm is really going to help you grow your account and your website.

Step 1 : clean up your old pins

Let's do some spring cleaning. Delete any pins that are off-brand or irrelevant to your audience. This isn't necessarily part of the Smart Feed, but because of some things that we're going to be doing later on in this book, it is important that all of your pins are on point. So if you wouldn't pin it nowadays, delete it.

Now again, some later strategies involve re-pinning your old content, so we want to make sure your content is worth re-pinning. Now when I did this, going through my old pins, I found a lot of stuff where I was like "I pinned that? Like, why did I pin that?" I no longer share pins on "How to start a blog". My audience has moved way beyond that. My audience is there to dominate and succeed and already have blogging figured out.

You want to go through old pins on your boards and this is going to take a while, and just delete anything that's really off-brand, irrelevant or visually unappealing. Anything that just doesn't work, something that you wouldn't pin now, delete it. I would also kind of take a little bit of caution, I wouldn't go through and delete 1000 pins in one day because Pinterest might think what's happening to their account; is this spam, is this person a real person. They might flag your account if you go through and delete 1000 pins in one day. I recommend sticking to 100, 200 per day deleting your off-brand pins. No more than 100 to 200 per day and you should be totally fine.

Step 2 : delete pins with bad, broken links

If your pins lead to broken or irrelevant links, meaning it's leading to a website that has nothing to do with the pin itself, then this is going to lower your internal user ranking with Pinterest. Pinterest is looking for the highest quality pins and users to share.

Think of Pinterest, again, as you would Google. So when you type a search term on Google, you're not going to get irrelevant results. You're generally going to get the best content on the Internet that has to do with the thing that you typed into Google. Pinterest is becoming more like Google, so they want to only share the best content, too. If your boards are filled with pins that lead to irrelevant websites or that have broken links, then it's going to kind of demote your profile and make it so that your pins and your own content get demoted as well.

Pin Doctor is a pretty cool tool on BoardBooster. It will search all of your bad links, broken links, irrelevant links, duplicate pins etc., and it only costs one cent per pin to search for those, so super worth it. It basically just crawls your account and then finds any pin that it deems as irrelevant or unworthy of being on your account so that you can easily and quickly delete them.

Step 3 : add pin descriptions

Great images get people to re-pin the image, but great descriptions get people to click through to your website. This is also an opportunity for you to be a "related pin" or a "picked for you". If you've been around the Pinterest block for a little while, then you've probably seen in your feed, related pins or picked for you pins. They are labelled that way in your feed.

Basically, Pinterest is selecting pins that it thinks you will enjoy based on the other kinds of content you pin. **You could become that pin for someone else which is the whole point here**, but they're not going to find your pin unless you have **pin descriptions with keywords** in them. We're going to be talking about that a little bit more, but get that idea in your head that you have a big opportunity here to get in front of more people.

Now a trick for adding descriptions. You might have had the problem before where you weren't able to add a description, like there is a random description that's automatically added to your photos or your images from your website. If you are using WordPress, you can write a description that gets added to your images every time someone pins them. Even if some random person comes to your site, uses the pin it button and pins your image, that description that you wrote with those keywords and that call to action is going to be automatically embedded into the pin. This is pretty awesome.

You just add the description as the image's Alt text before you insert the image into the post. It doesn't work if you've already inserted the image, you need to go back, delete the image, reinsert it or add the Alt text and then reinsert it into the post, and then you're always going to have that description when somebody, anybody pins from your site. So now every pin from your site will have a description rather than like cute-summer-dress.jpeg or the post title or something that's totally irrelevant.

Step 4 : get people to pin your content

The first person who should be pinning your content is you. You want to pin your own content first which honestly I thought was the weirdest thing when I first started doing it. I felt like I was self-promoting and just being a big Pinterest weirdo by pinning my own content, but you **should** be pinning your own content. You don't want to solely rely on other people to do it for you.

Second, add a pin it button to your website. The one that I recommend for WordPress users is jQuery Pin It button for Images, but whether you are on WordPress or Squarespace or any kind of website, you can use a plug-in to add a pin it button to your website which makes it really easy for people to pin your images for you.

You can also promote your pins in certain Facebook groups. Be careful because you don't want to spam in a Facebook group that doesn't allow these types of promotions, but there are some Facebook groups that you can seek out that are specifically for sharing your Pinterest images and getting people to re-pin them. You might want to search for some of those Facebook groups to help some of your pins gain traction quickly.

You also may want to add a Pinterest widget to your relevant blog posts and your sidebar. A Pinterest widget is basically this little Pinterest box that you can add inside of your blog content or on your sidebar, or anywhere on your website and it shows your Pinterest board with your pins and it has a follow button so people can see the types of content that you pin and they can also follow your Pinterest account.

Let's say you have a blog post that you wrote about healthy eating, how to eat healthier and you have a board on Pinterest called "Healthy Eating". It would be perfect to embed that Pinterest board widget into your blog post and tell people "if you really enjoy this blog post, why don't you follow me on Pinterest?" It makes a sense, so that is another option for you to use as well. Now you can add a Pinterest widget by simply going to one of your boards on your Pinterest account and there's just a little button you can select to grab that code for the Pinterest widget and place it on your website. And lastly, you want to add keyword rich descriptions to all of your pins on Pinterest. We're going to be talking more about this, but I want to reiterate it because it's a huge point in this book.

Why is it so important to get people pinning your content? Well, Pinterest has something now called Aggregate Re-Pin Numbers, which means the pins show the total number of re-pins among all Pinterest users, rather than just a number of re-pins that that particular user received.

Now this is a good thing because before, your pins would be scattered around people's profiles and most of the time, they would only have one or two pins. They just have a handful of pins really, because those users weren't getting a lot of repins on your content or any content, but not because they have these aggregate pin numbers which show the total re-pins, they look pretty beefed up which adds a whole lot of social proof, meaning when someone sees this pin that says 2.4 thousand re-pins, they immediately think, "That sounds like a pretty good article, maybe I should read it. It seems like a lot of other people are interested in it. I want to re-pin it!" These are the thoughts that people are having, but if they saw this pin and it only had two re-pins, they might not really have that same reaction.

Having these total re-pin counts on your pins does give it an element of social proof which is why you should encourage all of your followers to pin your content. Every single pin counts at this point because it all goes towards that total re-pin number rather than just having those scattered one or two re-pins on your followers' different accounts.

Step 5: be consistent

The Smart Feed rewards users who pin consistently and often, so you want to be consistent on Pinterest. It's important to pin between 50 and 100 pins per day which I know sounds insane, but don't worry because eventually looping will once again be a feature (once exclusive to BoardBooster, soon to be available with Tailwind), which will cut down on your pinning time. Or, you can use Tailwind to schedule. I'm not kidding.

Now, I cannot stress enough how important these steps are. This is what will help you become a high-quality pinner stat. We really want Pinterest to realize that you are a high-quality user, that you care about Pinterest, and that you are sharing awesome information. But if you're not following the steps in this section, then it's going to be hard for Pinterest to rank you highly in their feed. I can't stress enough how important these steps are.

JUST TO RECAP...

• The Smart Feed is Pinterest's algorithm that you can outsmart.

• You want to clean up your old pins, add pin and board descriptions and be a consistent pinner if you want to see great results on Pinterest.

10 SEARCH ENGINE OPTIMIZATION

40% of pinners have a household income of $100k+

Now let's talk about adding SEO to your pins and boards. So what exactly is SEO? What does this stand for? It stands for Search Engine Optimization which means that it helps your content appear at the top of the feed or search results. The same thing goes for Google. So the post that you see at the top of Google search results whenever you search for something, typically have strong SEO. In this section, I'm going to show you how to get stronger SEO on Pinterest. A major component of SEO is using relevant keywords that your target audience is searching for, so keep that in mind as we talk about SEO.

Your profile name which we talked about in one of the earlier sections, your pin descriptions and your board descriptions, and bonus, you should also be using it off of Pinterest inside of your content and with your content's title on your actual website. So you've got a few different places that you should be using keywords and the more that you pump up the keywords in these different locations, the better results you are going to get on Pinterest. It's really that simple.

Starting off with your profile name, you can see that in my profile I put my actual name, but then I put a little column and then I wrote some keywords. These are keywords that are designed to attract the people that I serve. I want you to add keywords to your profile name on Pinterest as well. This is going to make your profile more searchable, and it has another effect because now when people see your profile, they're going to see those keywords right up front and center as soon as they get to your profile.

This is a good thing because the people who should be on your profile, your target audience that you are trying to attract. If they see those keywords, they are immediately going to resonate with them and they are going to feel like, "Oh I found an incredible account that I really love that gets me." It's going to repel the people who aren't right for you, which is an equally good thing because the worst thing you can do is grow a big audience full of people who don't give a crap about your brand. We can simultaneously attract the right people and repel the wrong people by simply adding keywords to your profile name.

Now step two is to add keywords to your pin descriptions. Pinterest has limited your descriptions to only about 50 characters. You can see here that my pin description actually gets cut off a little bit and this is all I can really fit on my pin. You want to add keywords to your description. You don't really have a whole lot of room so you can't really write sentences or anything like that, but you can add some words that people might be searching for in order to find that particular pin.

So think about what would your target audience be searching for in order to find this pin and how can you add some keywords to your pin's description to lead those people to that pin. Now you may also want to consider which keywords you want to rank for. For example, if you're a real estate agent in Atlanta, then you're probably pretty location dependent.

You're not going to be helping people find houses in New York City because you live in Atlanta and you probably help people in the real estate market where you live.

In that case, you probably want to rank for keywords like real estate agent Atlanta, so I would add those keywords to every single pin of yours that you share on Pinterest. Now that's just one example. You may want to rank for pins for a variety of reasons, maybe you sell a product or maybe your blog is very specific on a certain topic so you want to rank for those specific keywords. You can add the same keywords to all of your pins in order to really build up that momentum with those keywords for your content. Remember, be straightforward. No flowery language here my friends. Your keywords should be very straightforward, to the point.

For example, if you sell Bohemian jewelry, try keywords like "handmade jewelry, Bohemian jewelry or Bohemian style", because all of these are things that people might be searching for on Pinterest and they are designed to attract your target customers, or maybe you are a graphic designer. Try keywords like "graphic design, logo design or feminine website". Again, these are the types of things that people might be searching for in order to find a graphic designer, maybe they're looking for someone to design their website for them.

So they would be typing different things like this into Pinterest. Maybe you blog about getting out of debt, so you could try keywords like "how to get out of debt, financial tips or how to save money". Again, these are the types of things that people would be typing into Pinterest's search bar in order to find your content or your products.

Lastly, you want to add keywords to your board descriptions. It is no mistake that this particular board on my account is my most popular board. This board tends to get the most re-pins, the most impressions and the most followers because look at all those keywords. I've got a bunch of keywords to attract people to this board, so if they are searching for these keywords on Pinterest or sometimes even on Google, they will find this board. It's a great way to attract people to your pins, your boards and your profile by simply adding keywords that they would be searching for anyways.

Now just like your pins, you want your boards to have keyword rich descriptions. I would brainstorm 10 to 15 keywords or phrases and add them to your board descriptions. This is again going to help your boards pop up in search results or be that coveted "picked for you" board. "Picked for you" is basically when Pinterest picks your board and puts it into somebody's Pinterest feed.

They don't have to be following you because Pinterest selected your board out of all the other boards because you've got rocking SEO and they can tell, so they are going to put you in other people's Pinterest feeds which is going to increase the likelihood that people are going to follow that board or re-pin the content from that board. This is a very big deal and another reason why you want to add keywords to your board descriptions because otherwise, maybe Pinterest won't know what that board is about.

And lastly, Pinterest boards can actually pop up in Google's search results. Not only will you be able to pop up in Pinterest search results, but you will be able to pop up on Google, too, if you have good Pinterest SEO, so we're killing two birds with one stone here.

Now altogether: adding keywords to your profile name, your pin descriptions and board descriptions makes your account and content searchable which is huge, because without keywords no one will find your content. Think about that for a second because most Pinterest users do not do this, most Pinterest users do not do this, most Pinterest users don't even know that this is a strategy.

By adding keywords to your pins and boards and profile name, you are immediately jumping ahead of majority of Pinterest users out there. This ends up resulting in huge gains and quick wins against other Pinterest users. After filling your account with keywords, you're going to begin to shoot up to the top of people's feeds which means more followers on Pinterest, more traffic to your website and more email subscribers.

JUST TO RECAP...

• Your Pinterest growth relies heavily on SEO and keywords

• You want to use keywords in your profile name, your pin descriptions and your board descriptions

• Put it all together and this will help your content to be found and shared on autopilot and like crazy

11 GROUP BOARDS

72% of Pinners use Pinterest to decide what to buy offline.

I n this chapter, we're talking about group boards, your new secret weapon. But first, what is a group board?

What is a group board ?

So someone owns the board, the group board and invites other people to pin to it. They are the owner of the board, they created it and then they can invite people to pin to that board. So some group boards have two people pinning to it and some have 200. It really depends on the board, but somebody owns it and then they invite other people to pin to it. Any pin shared to that board are shown to anyone following it, so not necessarily your followers. So the pins that are shared on that board are only shown to the people who are following that group board, so not people who are following your Pinterest account.

First, a History Lesson on Group Boards

Before 2014 came around, Pinterest developed group boards to get the concept of community posting going. The concept involved multiple people sharing content on the same board. Marketers and bloggers used group boards as a mechanism to get their content in front of new audiences, which was an advantageous move on their part, and still is today.

In 2014, the Pinterest algorithm changed to what we have today, but of course, over the years the algorithm has evolved with new updates pretty much on a quarterly basis. The feed has since changed from a chronological standpoint to a smart feed, where only the best pins show up in the feed. In 2015, many of the group boards became utterly useless. Ever since then, there's been a focus and striving to try and figure out how to make group boards relevant again and work for marketers and Pinterest pinners like you and me.

Unfortunately, there is still a mindset out there among the Pinterest marketing groups to pin and spam the boards as much as possible to try to get the pins in front of as many people as possible. This is not at all a good strategy. Being part of boards that are not relevant to your brand or are filled with spam will hurt your account in terms of how the algorithm views you. Don't post pins in places where your "people" are not.

Things have changed drastically since 2014. Joining tons of group boards was once a great strategy for gaining followers and re-pins pre-2014, but not so much today. And with change, means you have to change your strategy. You could belong to over 50 group boards (don't do this) and yet, still not get followers or re-pins if the board isn't performing well as a group. If your group board has less than a 1% re-pin rate, it's not a good board to be on.

Why group boards ?

Why do we like them? They allow you to get your content in front of new people. So again, if you have say 300 followers, but you are joining a group board which has 3,000 followers, then your pins are going to be shared with 3,000 people, not just your 300 people.

That's awesome, right? If you join a group board that has a lot more followers than you, then you are basically increasing your number of followers without having to increase your number of followers. It's pretty awesome.

Group boards are going to increase your traffic and your re-pins. And they will also show others that you are a leader and authority in your niche. I always tell people to join group boards that are specific to their niche.

For my business, I wouldn't join a group board for recipes because that's so irrelevant to the content that I create. Even if I could get a lot of click-throughs to my website or something, I wouldn't do that. You want to join group boards that are very relevant to your niche, and it's going to set you apart because you are constantly pinning to all of these different group boards in your niche. You are getting in front of different audiences and different followers. Now they are not the end-all, be-all, but they are helpful to growing your Pinterest profile and driving traffic (for free!) to your blog and business.

How I evaluate group boards

First, I look for the name of the group board to ensure it's relevant and meaningful (does it have keywords and is it using funny charac-ters or unnecessary spaces between the board heading name?) and at the number of contributors to a group board. This is your best indica-tion of the overall health of the group board. Then, I look at the number of contributors. If there's a group board with over 500 contributors, chances are the group board has become a "free-for-all" and is beyond any group moderator's ability to control. In addition, unmanaged groups have a higher risk of spam or irrelevant content, and out-of-control boards are not a place you want to be.

Finally, I look at the content. Do I want my audience to see the content of the group board? If it's not a board filled with relevant and meaningful content for my own audience to see, it's not a board I want to be affiliated with.

The Evaluation Process - is the board working for you?

I evaluate my group boards about once a month using Tailwind. Another quick way to evaluate is to look at your Pinterest analytics and check out the boards with top pin impressions. My font board has always dominated this and I think it's just because... people really like fonts. Hmmm.

Another super helpful tool that Tailwind offers is the pin inspector. It's the best way to get really specific information on how your pins are performing because it shows you how many pins you added to any given board and adds up your re-pins you received during the timeframe selected.

Step 1: finding relevant group boards

Option one is to search for a specific keyword on Pinterest and then filter by boards. You want to look for boards with multiple Pinterest pinners, and you might have to click through to different boards to see if there are multiple pinners on that board.

Unfortunately, Pinterest makes it a little bit difficult for you to figure out if it's a group board or not, but luckily, there is a website, called pingroupie.com, which allows for you to search for a specific keyword just as you would on Pinterest, but it shows you only group boards from that topic. You can go through pingroupie.com and find boards on a topic that fits your niche and attracts the target audience you are trying to reach. It also has good engagement. So then you can click through from pin-groupie to those boards and then request to join them. That's a little bit easier.

Now a quick tip is if there are pinners that you love that are in your niche, that attract the people that you want to reach, go to their profile on Pinterest to see which group boards they are a part of. You can see if you go to someone's profile, you can see a group board is indicated by the little two-person icon. Look for that on these Pinterest profiles to see if any of the people you admire or have an audience you want to reach if they are part of any group boards and then you can request to join those group boards because they are probably working well for that person if they are part of that group board if they are seeing success.

Step 2 : selecting the best group boards

Joining boards can take a fair amount of time, effort, communication, and tenacity. Prepare yourself for rejection and not getting your request responded to. This is very common in mis-managed groups or for group board managers who have a hard time telling people "no, you're not a good fit". They'll most likely ignore your request and move on. But don't be discouraged!

Respect their rules—their board, their rules. If you're trying to join the board of an influencer, respect the rules of connecting with them. Pin their content, join their Facebook group, etc. This is your opportunity to demonstrate to them you're able to follow rules. If they say they aren't accepting any more users, respect that, move on, don't get butthurt over it, and don't harass them.

If they haven't left instructions on how to join the board, you can try contacting them through a Facebook group, their Pinterest profile, email, or their website. If you know someone who is a contributor to the group board, you can check and see if they can add you to the group. But first, be absolutely sure it's a board you want to be a part of.

The best way to find the "rules" of contact to join the group board as a contributor is to check the group board description and see if they've left any instructions about how to join. For some groups, it took 2-3 months before I was let in. Some board owners want to watch you first to determine whether or not you're a spammer. They'll watch your activity for a while first before letting you in.

Again, you don't want to join just any group board, you want to join the best ones, and joining 30 group boards is going to look spammy because these group boards are also going to be on your profile. I would recommend putting them at the bottom of your profile because they are not your board unless you own the group board, but they are not your boards so you don't want them to be the first thing that somebody sees when they come to your account.

I always put them at the bottom, but having 30 or even 10 kind of looks spammy, so at most aim to join five excellent boards. Now here is what the best boards have in common, and this is what I want you to look for when you are either on pingroupie or you are searching for boards on Pinterest to join:

• They are frequently pinned to. This is probably the most important thing because you want other people to be constantly pinning to these boards because if they are not, it means that you can't pin them consistently. You hopefully want people to be pinning to these boards all throughout the day so that you can pin to the board every day and it doesn't look spammy because if you are pinning every day and nobody else is pinning, then it's all going to be the stuff that you've pinned and that's going to look kind of spammy and just not very good. So you want it to be frequently pinned on so that it's easier for you to share your content on those boards without looking spammy.

• Pins on the best boards have an average of three or more re-pins. If you check out a group board and you notice that most of the pins have like one re-pin, zero re-pins, then it is probably not worth your time because this group board is not getting very much traction. You really want to look for group boards that have an average of three or more re- pins. I say average because some of them might have one re-pin or zero re-pins, but then others will have five or seven or ten, so on average, you want to have three or more re-pins, ideally, even five or more, but let's say three or more just to give them the benefit of the doubt.

• Pinners share quality content on the best boards. If you go through these best boards and it just looks like spammy, buy my product, visit my blog kind of stuff, then you know that it is not quality content. You want to look for group boards where people are sharing a mix of other people's content and their own content, and they are really searching for that high-quality content to share, because group boards are not immune to the smart feed. They need to have quality content as well to really pop up in the smart feed too. You want other people to be sharing quality content, and that's also going to show you that the people who are following that group board are quality followers because quality followers are not going to be following spammy group boards. So you want to make sure the other pinners share quality content. Also, you want to make sure the board is highly relevant to your main niche and the core of your brand. So again, just going back to your focus and choosing group boards based on your main focus or topic.

Now you can also use your Pinterest Analytics which we are going to get into in a later section, but you can use your Pinterest Analytics with group boards. If we go to your Pinterest profile, you can see that highlighted at the top, and then we take a look at impressions and scroll down, you're going to see a section like this that says boards with top impressions. Now this is going to show you which group boards you joined that are giving you the best benefit.

Step 3 : creating a schedule

I pin all my content to my own boards first. I pin all the stuff from my blog to my own boards, typically my brand board so I pin there first. From there, I re-pin my content to my group boards at a 1:1 ratio.

I rank my group boards by performance. When I create a new blog post, I pin it to my best boards first and intersperse pins to my group boards. I use group boards as a supplement, not as my main strategy. Avoid being "spammy" on a group board—for managed group boards, spammy activity will get you kicked out.

For each pin of mine that I pin to a group board, I pin one of somebody else's too. You don't just want to go to a group board and pin only your own stuff, that's going to look spammy and it's just not really cool. You want to make sure that you are pinning other people's stuff too.

Now check your group boards every day to see if you can pin to them, so multiple times a day if they are particularly active. Again, that's why it is important group boards are pinned to frequently because you want to be able to pin to them frequently too. The more often people are pinning to them, the more often you can pin to them without looking as spammy.

Now I don't share more than three pins at a time because again, you don't want to look spammy. I can share a couple of mine and one of somebody else's and call it a day. Now if this sounds like a lot of work, checking your group boards every day, I know that that can sound like a lot of work, stay tuned for the next section because you can schedule all of this.

There is a way that I'm going to show you how to do this where you don't even have to schedule it, it just – it's basically automatic, takes me like 30 minutes a week to do all of my Pinterest scheduling, 100 pins a day – it's crazy. But good.

Number of Group Boards vs. Personal Boards

There's no magic answer to the question of what is the perfect ration of personal boards to group boards. The answer simply does not exist. I have five times the amount of personal boards to my group boards, because I want the focus to be on my content and content I find relevant to my audience.

Never neglect your personal boards for the sake of trying to "win it big" with group boards. Personal boards typically perform better than group boards because you are the owner of those boards and have complete control over everything that is posted in them.

Number of Group Board Followers

Students in my Pinterest Strategy course often ask whether boards with a lot of followers are better than boards with fewer followers. Here's my take on this. You want to join boards with people who have close to the same audience size as you do, meaning around the same amount of followers on Pinterest (not on the group board—the group owner's account). This is why open group boards don't really work. Open group boards tend to accept everyone, including people who do not yet have an established presence on Pinterest. Meaning, they haven't put in the hard work yet.

Content Sharing Options

We've talked about group boards in great length, but it's important not to forget about Tailwind Tribes and Facebook share and pinning threads and groups. Is it necessary to use all of them? Is one of them better than the other? Which ones provides the most benefit?

I typically don't participate in Facebook share threads (like pin 10 of the comments and like each one you pinned and share your link below) and I avoid them like the plague if they require you to share every pin that's being posted in the thread. Again, I don't need recipes or baby clothes on my pin boards. You want to pick and choose the content you're most likely to share with your blog audience.

With Tailwind Tribes, you have the opportunity to choose what content you want to share which is a huge benefit, but the downside is that not all the tribes, especially free-for-alls, may not have "quality" content that matches your boards' aesthetics, or even relevancy to your subject matter. Tribes do have the benefit of being able to monitor whether or not people are following the basic rules of the tribe, though, another benefit.

When should you start your own group board?

Only when you have a small group of people with content that you know you want to share with your audience would you want to start a group board. You technically only need one other person to start a group board, but to get listed on PinGroupie you need a minimum of five. Then there's no pressure as far as managing that board, and you get to set the rules. It's all about collaborating with people you know and ensuring all of you are generating relevant and good content. This is simply a "back to the basics" approach to starting a group to collaborate and curate content with.

JUST TO RECAP...

- Group boards can get your pins in front of much larger audiences, so if you have a small audience and you join a group board with a big audience, you can get your pins in front of much more followers.
- It is important to find relevant group boards with a high re-pin rate and lots of activity.
- Use your Pinterest Analytics to see which group boards are delivering the best results and you can also see which ones are delivering the worst results so that you can remove the boards that are not doing well. So if you are part of some boards that are giving you the lowest amount of impressions or re-pins, then you know that you can leave those boards because they are just not really helping you. Now go to pingroupie.com or go to Pinterest and search for some keywords to try and find some group

boards that are going to be awesome and help you reach a larger audience.

- Group boards can perform well for you provided that they're the right fit for your account. It's not all gloom and doom if the boards you really want to be in are full. If you are evaluating your group boards and find it's time to leave, just know that no one gets a notification if you leave the group board. I've left plenty of groups that became mis-managed and out of control. I've even left some boards where I was pressured by the boards' creator to have me write articles about her Etsy business on my own blog, even though it wouldn't be relevant to my audience, just to be part of her group board. And if you leave the group board, don't worry about automatically joining a new one.
- Group boards can be helpful but you're going to get a lot more impact for your account on things you can actually control: those two things are your image content and your keywords.

12 SCHEDULING AND LOOPING PINS

1 of 2 millennials uses Pinterest every month.

In this chapter, we're going to be talking about scheduling and looping your pins using Tailwind. BoardBooster's software program, when it was still in operation, had a feature called "looping", which would "recycle" your older pins and re-pin them automatically over time. So if you hear about the term "looping pins" this was originally a BoardBooster feature that Tailwind has adopted. Looping can help you make 100 re-pins of your choosing every single day. So when this feature becomes available again in another platform such as Tailwind, it'll be important for you to use it. I schedule with Tailwind because I have to pin stuff from my tribes. I can see the pins and the times they'll be scheduled, and also check a ton of analytics. Each program offers something different.

It's the looping feature in BoardBooster that was the original the game changer.

Now using Tailwind and BoardBooster combined, I grew my

following to over 4000 Pinterest followers in one year and it's continuing to grow right now at a rate of about 100 to 200 followers per month. Since that time, BoardBooster has shut down. Many users have turned to Tailwind. There's been a lot of discussion about whether the cost of Tailwind with Tribes is worth it. Many pinners have noted in the Facebook groups that they're not seeing the value of Tailwind tribes, so you'll have to make that sort of decision for yourself.

At the moment, my account is growing at about 5-10 new followers per day, I really want you to see that same success and that's why I am sharing both Tailwind and other options with you because they are time-saving programs. My page views have doubled and has kept me at 100k+ page views per month consistently, and with my Pinterest following growing with the number of re-pins that I'm making growing, my visitor and page counts have doubled as well, and my email list is starting to surge even more.

I only need to use Pinterest for about 30 minutes per week. So you might be thinking like wow, that's a lot of results but is it going to take me forever? And honestly, I'm using Pinterest a lot less time-wise than when I was using before, so it's incredible how time-saving it is and how effective it is. I'm all about finding things that are time-saving and effective.

Get this, it only costs me $35 per month for Tailwind. I was "grandfathered" in as an alpha user with Tribes, so I receive different pricing than a new customer. I don't know if $35-$70 per month is cost prohibitive to you, depending on if you choose to buy the power-ups that Tailwind offers. Hopefully since you're reading this book that will be an expense that you can manage, but even if you can't, there are different plans so you could start at even five dollars per month. Use my codes and invites at the front of the book so you can get moving without any expense incurred straight away.

Scheduling with Tailwind

Remember that first function we talked about, scheduling. So instead of pinning all your pins at once, you can schedule them to be pinned later on. Remember – I primarily use Tailwind for my scheduling just because I have to satisfy the sharing requirements for my tribes.

Looping boards

My absolute favorite feature. It's not yet available in Tailwind, but they are working on it. It's going to re-pin your content from your boards, starting with the oldest content first. This is awesome because it gives new life to your old pins. Remember those pins that are just sitting there? It also increases re-pin rate as your following grows. If you have 200 followers right now and then as you start implementing all these strategies from this book, maybe you grow to 1000 followers. Those pins that you shared when you had 200 followers probably don't have as many re-pins because you didn't have as big of an audience to share them to.

As your audience grows, you can use this looping feature to re-pin those old pins and now all those thousand people or thousand followers are going to see your pins again, re-pin them. Then it also has this cool feature, so after X amount of days it deletes the pin with the lower amount of re-pins. You can imagine with looping where it's repinning your old content, you're going to have two of the same pin on one board. Now you might think, like are people going to notice or is it going to be obvious, but really it's not, because you probably pinned that first version of the pin several months or even a year or so ago.

So, generally, people are just not going to notice. I've never had anyone tell me that they could tell that I've pinned the same pin three months later. Don't worry about that. This keeps your board active without you needing to constantly find pins to schedule, and that's why it saves me so much time because I don't have to go through and find 100 pins per day to schedule like you would have to do with other scheduling programs or if you're just doing it by yourself with no program, it's going to take forever. With looping, you don't have to do that, you just keep your boards active by using content you've already pinned. Genius!

Again, the looping feature is yet to come back to our pinning community at the date of publication. It will be exciting to have it back to help us all as a pinning community .

Best time to pin

Because of the smart feed, there really is no "best time to pin". But I will say that most pinners are on Pinterest in the evening, Saturday morning, and Saturday night, according to trends I've discovered in using various services.

I make sure that I do some organic pinning around that time as well. I schedule, I (used to) loop but then I also do pin some things myself, I just go on Pinterest and pin a few things in the evening because that's when my audience is online.

You can absolutely sign up with these other programs too but just know that you can't loop pins as far as I know, and looping pins is a thing that has really saved me the most time because I can pin 100 pins per day and not have to find 100 things per day.

If you are scheduling pins, you're going to have to find a lot of stuff every day and that's going to take a lot of time. So that's why don't use the other ones but I do know some people who like them so you could check them out.

JUST TO RECAP...

• Clean up your pins and boards. Basically you just want to get your Pinterest profile already for the impact of monthly viewers, and you'll look like a pinning professional.

• Keep in the loop for the looping feature to return through pinning services software. I'll post it on my blog and update everyone when new features are ready.

13 CREATING ORGANIC PINS

Over 5% of all referral traffic to websites comes from Pinterest.

You learned how to use the scheduler to schedule pins to your group boards, and now in this chapter, I'm going to show you how to schedule organic pins. By organic pins, I mean the content that you are pinning onto your boards, your regular boards, not the group boards but the ones that you created for your profile.

Pinning organic pins is as easy as clicking the "+" button at the top of your Pinterest profile page, or using a scheduler to upload or obtain your image directly from a link to your website.

From there, you manually type in the pin description if you're uploading an image. If you're providing a link and have rich pins enabled, Pinterest will automatically draw in the link's initial content description. You would then save your pin to the board.

Using this process, I then click on my Tailwind Chrome extension button and schedule the pin to go to my tribes, as well as other board lists I've created within Tailwind. It really is that easy.

Tailwind has the capability to allow you to schedule pins to your boards so that they go out over the span of a few days or weeks which means that you can basically batch your pinning so that you just do it in one sitting and then you have content for weeks or months depending on how much you've actually scheduled.

You can schedule pins in advance for blog posts you haven't published yet or made available using Tailwind. This is especially helpful if you want to take a break from social media (always a good thing to do every other week). Or, if you have vacation planned and still want new content to go out, use the Tailwind scheduling system to get your blog posts out and no one will know you're out of town.

14 PINTEREST ANALYTICS

Pinterest said 80% of its users access Pinterest through a mobile device.

I n this section, we're getting a little bit techy because we are analyzing your Pinterest Analytics.

Now just upfront a note, you must sign up for a free business account to access Pinterest Analytics. If you don't have a business account, you might be looking at this section and this section and kind of be wondering what the heck is going on. So make sure that you sign up for a business account. This is explained in an earlier section, but you should do it before proceeding, otherwise this is going to be gibberish to you. It's really easy to set up your account though. So just go back to the previous section where we talk about setting up your business account and you should be all good to go.

Before we get into this section, I need to tell you that talking about analytics is not the most exciting thing in the world. It's a little bit dry, not too fun, like some of the other chapters you've read, but it's essential to learn. Be sure you're logged into your Pinterest account so you can follow along.

Alright, so to view your analytics you go to your profile page and then click the little gear symbol on the top right and scroll down until you see analytics and click that. Remember you need a business account in order to access that. Now this is the landing page you're going to see, the Pinterest Analytics landing page. If you click more, next to any of those three boxes, it's going to take you to three different pages. It's important to have your Pinterest analytics pulled up on your computer while you read this so you fully understand.

First, we're going to be talking about your Pinterest profile, so let's click the more button next to your Pinterest profile and we can view the stats about your profile. Now just real quick, you can see that there are some different stats right here on the front page. I honestly don't keep too much of a track of these different stats. It's nice to know occasionally how many people are viewing your profile, how many people are viewing your pins, but you kind of want to see if these are increasing or decreasing by a lot, but I don't pay a lot of attention to these. I usually think it is best to just click through and look at the actual stats, the more specific stats than paying super close attention to these vague numbers.

Let's get to it, your Pinterest profile. Now these are the boards and pins that your followers enjoy the most. We want a healthy balance of clicks and re-pins which means that they are power pins. This is going to make a whole lot more sense once I show you the screen that your Pinterest profile analytics will take you to, but if they are not clicking then it's not creating viral sharing, and if they are only re-pinning, then no one is actually reading your content.

Now if we go to your Pinterest profile, that first little box, then we have top pin impressions. You can see there is a little navigation bar at the top, says impressions, re-pins, clicks and all time. If we click impressions, then we have some different columns there which also says impressions, clicks, re-pins, likes. I just like to take a look at this screen and it shows you your top pin impressions from the last 30 days. Now take note all of my top pin impressions are rich pins, and yours should be, as well. Don't worry, you'll get there.

You can see that on the farthest right corner where it says pin type, that box with an "R" in it, that means that they are rich pins. If you didn't believe me that rich pins are important, then girl or boy, because there's some boys in this course too, rich pins are very important. They show that you have a high-quality pin. I just want to point that out. And also, in case you're wondering what the "P" is, that means it's a pin that is promoted.

Now here's the big thing that I want you to pay attention to, that I was talking about in the previous slide. Compare your clicks versus your re-pins to craft better descriptions.

If I wanted to boost my re-pin rate, I could do a few different things. I could promote the pin to promote it to aim to get more re-pins. I could craft a better description that encourages people to re-pin, remember adding that call to action. So there are a couple of different things that you could do.

Now if any of them were getting, say, more re-pins and not so many click throughs, then that definitely means that I could create a better description to get people to click through the pin to actually visit my website. So again, creating a call to action like "click through to read the full article" or even creating a new pin image, just like my old one but adding a call to action button like we talked about in the pinnable pins section, where you're adding like little graphic on to your image saying click through or click to read or something like that where you're encouraging people to actually click through and read your article. Because it's nice to have re-pins but it's not so nice if people actually aren't clicking through to read your article. Those are just a few different things you can do by analyzing this data, the top pin impressions.

Now we also have top board impressions if you scroll down. So these are the topics your audience loves. Now these are all of your boards, remember this is your Pinterest profile.

Take a look at your top boards, are they on brand, are they relevant to what you're trying to create, that focus that you are trying to create on your website. If I look at mine, they're pretty darn relevant because I'm aiming at bloggers and entrepreneurs. So we have 'blogging tips', 'entrepreneur tips', 'dream office', 'blogging tips and tricks resources'. There are a couple in there that are a little bit random like home decor or words which is like quotes, but most of them are pretty on-brand and relevant to my audience.

So I'm making sure that my top boards are ones that are going to attract my ideal audience. And again, create a call to action specific to your needs, re-pins versus clicks. So depending on which boards have a lot of clicks versus re-pins, remember you want a healthy balance of both, trying to create those descriptions on the pins within that board, that are going to kind of up the clicks if you're low on clicks or up the re-pins if you're low on re-pins.

For example, my 'home office inspiration' board, the very bottom almost, home office inspiration board has hardly any clicks but it has quite a lot of re-pins. So I could create different kinds of descriptions to really add that call to action and get people to click through and read more of those posts because it's really not doing any good to pin things that board because people aren't clicking through to the actual post and reading them.

Now if you click all time at the top, you can see which pins rank the highest in search, so best in search, pins that rank higher in search. What do these pins have in common? Now these aren't necessarily my pins, pretty much none of these pins are from my actual website, they are just pins that I pinned, but take a look at the pins that show up in this best in search section, because these pins are the ones that are power pins according to Pinterest, ones that are doing really well in search, that something about these pins someone is doing right.

Now moving on to the second section, your audience. Your audience section only has two subsections; demographics and interests. If we click the very first one that says demographics, it shows us basically where our followers and our pinners, our audience is coming from; so which countries, which cities, what languages and what gender. So as you can see, most of my audience comes from the US and specifically Los Angeles or big cities in general, and also most of my audience is female.

These kinds of demographics can be really helpful especially if you have like a product based business where you are shipping things out, maybe you see that a lot of people are re-pinning your stuff from the UK, but you don't ship to the UK. So maybe you want to change that because currently, you have a big market for the UK but if you're not shipping to them then you could be losing out on a lot of business. Taking a look at your demographics and just seeing if there is any way that you could incorporate these demographics into your blog or business.

Now if you click the interests section next to demographics, it's going to take you to a screen. This shows your interests, what your audience is into. These are the topics that your peeps are searching for the most. So for most of them, what I write about fonts and designs, that's kind of all clumped together under graphic design. There isn't really a great topic to pick for that one but I have to pick graphic design, there is like a robot or something there which is why graphic design is so high on mine, but this represents the whole view of your target market, beyond just what you are selling.

I might write about blogging, social media tips, but my audience is also really interested in home decor, recipes, home improvement, inspirational quotes etc. So it kind of just gives me a more in-depth picture of who my audience is so that I can create like a brand story around my brand which really appeals to my audience. Now I don't recommend taking these interests and then pinning about all of them or blogging about all of them, that's just going to ruin your blog's focus or your business' focus, but rather I just want you to take a look at these interests and see how they all come together to create this unique type of person.

Now under the interests section as well, we have this really cool part where it says boards: pinner boards with lots of your pins. These are basically boards that other people have created that tend to have a lot of your own pins on them. I think this is an awesome little analytics section that Pinterest provides you because it shows the top people who really dig what you are doing.

These could be people that you could reach out to, to collaborate with or maybe they are your ideal customer. So if you are selling something and they are constantly pinning your products, then maybe you could get like an ideal customer profile from them, really analyze who this person is, how you can add their interests to what you are selling or what you are creating. So study these people.

What can they teach you? Who are they? What's their job? Where do they live? What do they do? Why do they care so much about what you are putting out there? You can also find most likely on brand content to pin from these boards. If you are running out of things to pin or you are looking for awesome content in a pinch, then you can probably go to these boards under your audience interests boards and find a lot of cool stuff to pin that's totally on brand because most of these boards, it looks like talk about blogging business tips which is so central to my brand. So it would be really easy for me to just peek through all these boards and schedule a bunch of stuff onto my Pinterest.

Now lastly, we have audience interests: brands. These are the businesses your audience engages. Generally, these are your big name competitors, so what do they say about your audience. These are kind of like who you would be in 10 years, not 10 years, one year, two years – 10 years is crazy talk. These are your big name competitors. So what do they say about your audience? What can you glean from studying these competitors?

Now we're going to check out the last section, activity from your website. We have impressions, re-pins, clicks, original pins, all time – we have all this stuff. Try clicking on "impressions". We have top pin impressions and boards with top pin impressions. Now remember, these are just the pins from your website, not just things that you pin, but specifically things from your website. It shows you the top pins from your site with the most impressions, re-pins and clicks.

Now you can use this to analyze which types of content drive the most traffic. This is an awesome way to study your content, what you are putting on Pinterest, to see if people like what you write about often or maybe you'll see a post in there that you didn't even know people really liked or that really got a lot of traction on Pinterest, but all of a sudden, it's one of your top pin impression pins of the last 30 days and you are like, "oh wow maybe I should write more content like that, because clearly people are liking it". It could surprise you to see what you find on these, the top pin impressions or boards with top impressions.

Boards with top impressions similarly will show you what your audience, the specific topics that they really enjoy learning about. So definitely take a look at this, the activity from your website and then impressions to see what people are really falling in love with the most.

Now most re-pins, if we take a look at the column where it says re-pins, most re-pins generally mean that that type of content or that post inspires users. They don't necessarily need to click through to read it, but they want to save it for later because they aspire to be like whatever that post is selling. Now most clicks is indicative of users that want to learn more and/or are ready to buy.

So maybe they really want to learn about that topic or you are talking about a product and they are like I need that, so they click through to either read your article or buy your product. It is important to kind of take into account clicks versus re-pins because you want to see, are people just aspiring to be like this, they will save it for later, for one day or are they actually clicking through to take action today because we really want them to take action, we do want re-pins, but we don't just want re-pins. Take a look at your post, see which ones are getting clicks, see which ones are getting re-pins and see which ones are just getting the most impressions overall.

Some examples

If you have a product pin with lots of re-pins, but not as many clicks, so it's getting re-pinned a lot, but people aren't clicking through to read it, then here are a couple of things you need to do. You need to work on your pin's description, so add keywords to target the people who would want to click through. So maybe your description is lacking, maybe the people who your product pin is geared towards can't find your pin because it doesn't have the proper keywords in the description. Add those key words so that the right people are finding it. And then add a call to action to your pin image and your pin description. You're going to have to create a new image and then re-pin it if you want to do that route, but creating a call to action to your image and your pin description, like "click through to check out this product" or "click through to read the full article".

Now if you have a valuable blog post with lots of clicks but few re-pins, so every time somebody sees this blog post, they click through to read it, but most people are not re-pinning it, so not as many people are seeing it as could see it. If that's happening, lots of clicks but few re-pins, then add a call to action in the description encouraging people to re-pin it, like just tell them re-pin this post if you found it useful or re-pin this post and then click through to read or you could also promote your pin to get more re-pins, so promoted things as an option again, where you can promote it specifically to get more re-pins.

That could be a great option if you're getting a lot of clicks but few re-pins because it shows that you have a post that people really like, they probably click through to read it and then forget to re-pin it. So you just got to give them that call to action or try promoted posts to actually get them to see it more often.

Now lastly, we have best in search from your site. If we click all time and then we will scroll down and see best in search, these are the pins that rank higher in search. These are again power pins. Now which of your pins are ranking the highest? So again, thinking about the smart feed. These are the pins that always pop up at the top when somebody is scrolling through their smart feed. So why?

As you can see these all seem to have a description, so take a look, see what keywords you are adding and make sure that if you want a pin to pop up as best in search, you are adding those descriptions to your pins. So overall, your analytics will show you what your audience enjoys the most and the types of content you should create more of because clearly they love it, if there are any gaps in your content, so things that your audience is interested in but you are not providing. So things that they could like, maybe they fall under a certain topic but you just aren't really writing about them. And which pins could do better if you adjust the descriptions or pin images. Remember that call to action, re-pins versus clicks.

JUST TO RECAP...

• Sign up for a business account; you need your business account in order to access analytics.

• Explore your Pinterest analytics, so there are just tons of different things that you can take a look at. We covered most of them in this section, but really explore your analytics to see all the different stats that you have access to.

• Look for the content your audience enjoys most and then create more of it, super easy right?

• And then also look for the content that can be improved to better reach your goals. So basically just making sure that you are creating content that is hyper relevant and hyper useful to your ideal audience, so using your analytics to figure out what type of content that is.

15 USING GOOGLE ANALYTICS

93% of active pinners said they use Pinterest to plan for purchases and 87% said they've purchased something because of Pinterest.

———————

So whether you can consider yourself a data nerd or not, I have a feeling you're going to enjoy this section. We're talking about analyzing Pinterest using Google Analytics. Let's get started.

What is Google Analytics?

Google Analytics is a free analytics software which can tell you some pretty darn in-depth stats about your site. It can be really useful for seeing which pins are getting the most views and converting the most visitors into subscribers or buyers. If you don't have Google Analytics set up on your site already, I highly, highly suggest that you get on that.

How to install it

I'll just briefly go through how you can get Google Analytics on your site. It's really easy to do. It is very easy as you can tell. Visit google.-com/analytics, to create an account for your site.

Now when you create an account, you need to insert a tracking code on to your website from your Google Analytics account. That's how they kind of talk to each other. On WordPress, install the Google Analytics plug-in on your WordPress site. Then in Google Analytics, go to the admin > tracking info > tracking code and copy your tracking ID into the Google Analytics plug-in and you are done. It's super easy. If you are more familiar with the back end of a website, then you can do it without using this plug-in, but this is more of the simple way to add it to your website in case you are unfamiliar with more of the kind of back end of a website.

So this is the super easy way to add Google Analytics and then you can go to your Google Analytics account and pretty soon you'll start to see the stats rolling in. You can see how many visitors you are getting, which pages have the highest amount of page views. Those are really basic statistics, but Google Analytics can tell you a whole bunch of really interesting things about your site. So definitely get it.

Which posts get the most love?

This is one of my favorite ways to check out how Pinterest is doing on your site or with your site. To see which posts receive the most traffic from Pinterest, go to acquisition, social, overview and then Pinterest, so acquisition, social, overview, Pinterest – and from there, you can see which posts on your website or which pages on your website are getting the most traffic from Pinterest. This can be really useful for a lot of reasons. How to use this info? Why is it useful?

Now that you know which posts receive the most traffic from Pinterest, you can see what your audience enjoys the most and create more just like it. If you notice a trend that certain posts are getting more views than other posts from Pinterest, then you can make an effort to share more of those posts on your Pinterest account or even just pin the same images more than once; pinning them every week or every couple weeks because obviously your Pinterest followers like those types of posts.

Now if you sell products, this is also a great way to see which products you should create more of so that you can promote them on Pinterest. You can also add content upgrades and better paths in these posts to ensure that these visitors are going to stick around. You could also add more info about your products or affiliate links to generate more of an income.

Basically, once you know which posts are bringing the most traffic, then you just want to pimp out those posts. You need to add content upgrades, so adding a way for somebody to subscribe to your email list once they reach that post, and better paths, so what I mean by that is having more of a goal in mind with your post.

You could add affiliate links where you are getting people to come to that post and then they are purchasing something, so you make a commission or you are adding more info about your products or you are weaving in more back links to previous posts on your site to keep people clicking around more. So really think about what kind of paths you can add to your post. We talked about paths in a previous unit, but they are a really great way to think about what you want your visitors to do once they reach your post.

Now if this is an older post, which it might be because Pinterest is a search engine and SEO (Search Engine Optimization) usually takes a few months to really start booming. If this is an older post, then it makes sense because Pinterest sometimes takes a little while to really bring you a lot of traffic on those older posts. If it's an older post, update it to make sure it is evergreen and on brand.

You want to make sure that this is timeless content and that your images are on brand. I can't tell you how many posts I had to go back through and update because my images were just not looking good. They were from way back in the day when I had no idea what I was doing, but they are getting a lot of traffic because again, SEO takes a while to start booming. My older posts were starting to bring in more and more traffic because they've been around for a long time, but the images were just not very good. I updated those images, re-pinned those posts onto Pinterest so that I could now get traffic to that old image and to the new image that I pinned, so that post was doing even better than before.

Which pins work the hardest?

To see which pins drive the most traffic to your site – so before we were talking about which pages got the most traffic, now we are talking about which pins, specifically which pin images drive the most traffic to your site. To find that out, you go to acquisition, all traffic, referrals and then pinterest.com. It's going to take you to a page that looks like this, so we have the little referral path and you need to copy that path into your browser after pinterest.com. You can see that it's just the ending of the URL. You need to copy your referral path ending after pinterest.com and then you will be able to see which pin that is, the actual pin image will pop up. You can see which pin that is, to see which pin is driving the most traffic to your site.

How to use this information

Each of these referral paths is a pin that your visitors clicked in order to get your site. By visiting the links in the referral paths, you can see which pins are driving the most traffic to you. Now analyze these pins; do they have anything in common, are you targeting specific keywords in their descriptions, what do the images look like? See if there are any patterns.

Maybe you are surprised to find that a certain type of image is constantly bringing the most traffic or maybe they are all images with people in them or maybe it is a certain type of text that you tried out on your images or maybe it's just a certain topic. More likely, it's probably just a certain type of topic. So figure out which ones are bringing the most traffic to your site and if you can find any patterns in that data. Now knowing which pins work the hardest is a great way to make sure you create more pins and posts just like them.

JUST TO RECAP...

• Sign up for a Google Analytics account. You can easily sign up for an account within a matter of minutes.

• Add to the Google Analytics code to your site. There's a WordPress plugin that you can install as well to make it super easy.

• View which posts get the most love from Pinterest and that's going to tell you which types of posts you should create more of, which types of products your audience is really liking.

• View which pins drive the most traffic to your site so that you can create more pin images just like them and also pin topics on the same topic.

• And then use this data to enhance your content and Pinterest strategy, so pretty much just everything that we've gone through. Use that data to enhance your content and your strategies so that you can really bring in more of the right visitors.

16 DEVELOPING YOUR EMAIL LIST

Two-thirds of pins represent brands and products.

First of all why your email list is important? Because Pinterest is a fantastic way to help you grow your email list so I can't leave this out of the section. I got to tell you how you do it successfully.

Why your email list is so important

• Number one, it's direct. You can get in touch with your followers when you want to. You're not reliant on your audience checking their social media accounts or visiting your blog. You basically can get inside of their email inbox whenever you want. So if you have a new blog post up or you are running a sale or you have a new product that you are launching, this is a fantastic way to be able to get into their inbox so that they are seeing this new thing that you want to tell them about and they are not missing out on it, because if you just post it on your blog or your social media, there's a big chance that they are not going to see it. Getting in their inbox is a sure-fire way to make sure that they see your updates.

• Number two, you own your email list. Technically you don't own your following on social media and actually, you don't even own your following on Pinterest, but you do own your email list and it can't be taken away from you. People sign up to your email list and you have those people's names and emails that you can keep forever. You can continue to email those people even if Pinterest, Facebook, Twitter and Instagram all decide to close up shop. This is a really big deal because you want to make sure that if you're putting all of this effort into growing your blog or online business, that you have a tangible asset to be able to contact your followers and customers.

Facebook Crisis and Social Media Control

Now let me take you back to the big Facebook crisis that happened a few years ago. A few years ago, Facebook changed its algorithm for pages. Prior to changing its algorithm, you could post something on your Facebook page and it would just go bananas. People were getting a lot of traffic from Facebook, they were making sales. And then Facebook changed their algorithm, showing you that you do not own Facebook and now you're going to have to pay for Facebook ads if you want your content to be seen. So all those people who spent their time growing their Facebook page following were now left in the dust. I don't want that to happen to you which is why I think your email list should be the number one thing that you focus on growing.

So bottom line, no one can take your email list away from you. It's not dependent on algorithms or some other company's decisions. You should always be growing an email list in order to reach your audience and maintain your brand. Email lists are also more personal. A person's inbox is kind of like their virtual home. It means something when they invite you into it. It's almost like giving you their phone number, so they want to stay in contact with you and that is a big deal. When someone likes you on Instagram or likes your page on

Facebook, I don't think it means quite as much as somebody willing to give you their sacred email address. It also allows you to connect in a deeper way. So within your emails that you send to your list, you can connect to your audience in a more personal way.

You can share vulnerable stories. You can really get real with your audience. This allows the deeper connection and especially because you're reading them inside of their virtual home which just builds that connection even more, but it is overall more personal.

A fun fact: email lists have higher conversion rates than other types of things out there. If you are selling something or ever plan to, an email list is essential because it converts those people, potential customers into actual paying customers. Basically, bottom line, if you post the same offering on your Instagram, in a blog post and in an email, you will almost always get the highest percentage of buyers from your email. This should be a game changer alert for you if you are selling anything online.

JUST TO RECAP...

• Your email list is essential especially if you do or plan to sell something online.

• Develop your own email list and use it.

• It has higher conversion rates than social media and blog posts and it's proven to be an excellent place to connect with your audience.

17 CONTENT UPGRADES

Food & Drink and Technology are the most popular categories
for men.

Now if you want to grow your list, this section is going to be huge for you because we're talking about how to use content upgrades to grow your list with Pinterest.

What is a content upgrade?

Maybe you haven't heard this term before. A content upgrade is a download that you offer people in exchange for their email address. It upgrades a piece of content that you created by adding additional information for free. If that doesn't make sense, don't worry, I've got some examples for you.

Content upgrades can come in almost any form that you can think of; things like checklist, tutorials, workbooks, mini e-books, free email courses etc. Basically if you can think of a way to up level your content or add some extra value for your readers or visitors, then you can turn it into a content upgrade. Some examples are a free email course-now you can see I actually put a content upgrade on my Pinterest image to show people that if they click through, they're going to get access to this awesome freebie. Here we got my free email course. Here I created content upgrades that are spreadsheets. Here I created a free media kit and here is a free workbook, or a free cheat sheet. You can see that there are a number of different things that you can add for free as a content upgrade.

• You want to focus on providing extra value. Create something useful that helps people take action and gives them a way to dive deeper into your content because maybe they read your blog post or listened to your podcast or watched your YouTube video and they loved it, but now they want to know how do I actually put this into action or how do I take this to the next level. Your content upgrade is a way for you to add that extra value by letting people know that you've got a worksheet or a video or some other piece of content that's going to add extra value for them. It can also give even more content or tips.

• A pro tip: your content upgrade should always have a takeaway or end goal. What do you want someone to get out of this content upgrade that you're creating? What's the point of them signing up for it? So if you can answer that question, then you can be sure that you've created a really useful content upgrade.

How do content upgrades and Pinterest go together?

Here is the formula. Pinterest and everything you just learned in this book will drive a ton of traffic to your website. That's just the way it works. Then if you add content upgrades to your content, your podcasts, your blog posts, your videos, then that new traffic you're getting from Pinterest will then subscribe to your email list. It is amazingly effective and it runs on autopilot.

When I started doing this, I started implementing my Pinterest system, I started adding content upgrades to a lot of my blog posts, I grew my email list by about 8000 subscribers within one month. Within three months, I had grown my list more than 45,000 subscribers, and in 4 months of combining my Pinterest system with adding content upgrades, I grew my list to 50,000 subscribers. That's crazy, 3-4 months, 50,000 subscribers and it's largely due to this system that I just taught you.

How often should you create content upgrades?

Well adding them to every piece of content is ideal. That's what you want to shoot for, but obviously that's a pretty lofty goal and content upgrades can take a bit of time to create. Instead you can also reuse content upgrades on different blog posts or create something more general that you use all over the place. It's not just on one blog post or it's not just created for that particular blog post, but maybe you create a free email course or you create something that you can use on multiple blog posts and also in other places on your website. This is a great way to reuse your content upgrades but still get those people signing up to your email list from Pinterest.

Where to start

Where should you start if you have a lot of content, if you have no content? It doesn't matter. Where should you start with creating content upgrades? I recommend going straight to your most popular posts. This way you can capitalize on the posts that are already getting momentum and have a larger audience to convert because if you know that people are interested in these popular posts, then you know that they are probably interested in that topic. If you add on some sort of upgrade, worksheet, free email course, a cheat sheet, a checklist-whatever it is, then you can be pretty sure that people are going to be interested in it since they were already interested in the topic of that blog post.

After creating content upgrades for your 5 to 10 most popular posts, then you can begin creating content upgrades for new posts, but you want to start with those most popular posts because they are already getting traffic. Now to find your most popular posts, just go into Google Analytics and then search by behavior, site content, all pages. You can see it down there at the bottom. That's going to give you a list of your most popular posts on your website.

How do you create a content upgrade?

You could use a variety of design programs like Apple Pages or Microsoft Word, or you could do it in Adobe InDesign. It doesn't really matter which program you use, anything that allows you to save your content upgrade as a PDF if you're going to be sending some sort of worksheet. Otherwise, you could use your email service provider to send out something like a free email course or free video course, totally up to you.

How do you send this coveted content upgrade?

Well, you want to set up your email service provider so that your content upgrade is sent in the email that they receive after registering to your email list. This is super easy to do in MailChimp, and MailChimp is my recommendation to most people who are starting an email list or even people who are in this kind of intermediate level of using their email list because it has just the right amount of functionality for most people but it's still very easy to use.

JUST TO RECAP...

• Content upgrades are a very powerful way to grow your list with Pinterest.

• You create something that adds value to your content in order to gain subscribers.

Again, I use this same system to grow my list to 50,000 people in 4 months. So it can be done and it can be done fast.

18 BUSTING THE PINTEREST MYTHS

An average number of pins made by an active female user is 158.

Why Discuss Myths About Pinterest?

Time is precious. And when you're building your empire and using Pinterest to help market that special empire, you don't have time to mess around with rabbit holes or rumors that distract you and possibly steer you way off track. You want to get in, make an impact, create content, products, and make sales. There's no time to waste.

First 5 Pins of the Day - Now Retired

Pinterest has a tendency to change things every once in a while, so I've kept a page on my website that you will want to have book-marked on your computer in order to keep up with the changes.

A while back Pinterest experimented with a "first 5 pins of the day". They experimented with this a while before removing the feature in late June 2018. This is how their site explained it: "The first 5 Pins you save each day will be prioritized for distribution. Save to the most relevant board first." This was a crazy bit of change. Firestorms erupted, earthquakes happened, and the earth had a meltdown. Just kidding. But because this was such a confusing policy, with all of us trying to figure out when our "day" actually started based on time zones in conjunction with Pinterest's algorithm timezone, none of us were sure if the policy was going to have us pinning in the middle of the night and how much emphasis we had to put on it.

Like I said, they removed it. So if you're still hearing this myth that only the first five pins will be shown, please know that is no longer the case and you can stop pinning to that concept.

Followers

Is Pinterest now focusing on followers with the new "follower" button? Somewhat. Followers do matter, but they are not as important as you think, because remember, this is a search engine, not a form of social media. It's not the number of followers that matter to the Pinterest algorithm, but the engagement. Pinterest's algorithm focuses on how engaged your followers are with your content. You want an authentic audience, so as tempting as it is to buy followers for your Pinterest account, please know this will do absolutely NOTHING for you in terms of engagement or in rank on the Pinterest smart feed.

New Profile Look

Pinterest just released the new profile look for business accounts, where you can see specific pins from a board or your most recent pins. It's a beautifully-designed slanted pinning collage that a lot of us are pretty excited about. There was some initial confusion regarding the number of monthly viewers that is displayed in the new profile view. Should you pay attention to this? Yes. Absolutely, as it's the number of people who have seen your pins in the last 30 days. The purpose is so that you and the people visiting your profile (particularly group board managers and brand influencer decision-makers) can see just how far your influence reaches on Pinterest. Anyone with over 100k+ is considered to be a Pinterest power user.

Myths About Number of Pins Per Day & Pinning Habits

A good myth or rumor usually gets rolling by listening to only pieces of a topic on social media groups. Typically someone who believes they're an authority on the subject of Pinterest will experience something or hear other wrong information and share it with a crowd "making the information so". You're just getting bits and pieces of information. Like this one for example:

Provided you're keeping things relevant to your audience and spreading out your pins over time, you're good and there's no such thing as requiring daily activity or a specific number of pin quotas you need to meet. Pinterest wants fresh content. Don't pin the same things over and over again. You're not going to get the return you would like. Create multiple images for one piece of content to conduct some A/B testing and pin your new content to Pinterest as soon as possible after it's published.

Images

A lot of people feel like they have to go back through and update all their pins since Pinterest has changed up the sizing on images. The ideal size for a vertical pin has always been a 66% ratio or a 600x900. The Pinterest standard template size is 763x1102.

All the confusion started when Pinterest tried to eliminate confusion (funny, right?). The only thing changing is that pins longer than 1260 pixels will be cut off and not shown as much in the smart feed.

The best thing to do is figure out the kinds of images your audience likes the most. You can do this through trial and error, or, you can run some A/B testing of your pins.

One myth floating around is that if you use the same pin description on several pins, Pinterest will somehow "penalize" you in some way. Pinterest has not officially said this, but they do encourage the use of different descriptions to rank higher with SEO (search engine optimization).

Group Boards

It is completely false that you need to join group boards in order to be successful on Pinterest. This is just not the case. Who makes up these "rules", anyway? Sure, group boards do help provided they are relevant to your audience, but you do not "need" them in order to be successful.

Rich Pins

Myth: having rich pins enabled will negatively impact website traffic and conversion. I am going to address this myth from two perspectives. This myth was started by people who use recipe plugins and have rich pins enabled that were fearful that pinners will look at the information on the pin only instead of following it to the site. Basically, you can get the recipe right off of the rich pin without having to even visit the blogger's site.

Now, if this was true, it would be hurting users' traffic, and so far we as a Pinterest community have not seen rich pins negatively affect traffic. In addition, when you provide a great user experience, you get rewarded with a click-through. You have to really evaluate your user habits and determine if they're clicking through to your website.

As a user, however, I will confess that when looking for a recipe, I tend NOT to click through to the user's website to get the recipe when it's already included on the rich pin. Often times, I'm in a hurry to get dinner going and just need a quick idea. I don't need to know the history of the recipe, whether or not someone's family really enjoyed it, when the blogger typically makes it, etc. and to have to scroll through an endless page of ads with paragraphs of the recipe's story in-between, only to have to page through to get through the recipe. Perhaps it's just because I'm a seasoned Pinterest user and know that's what I'm going to experience practically ever single time I search for a recipe. So yes, I'm telling you, you're going to have users just like me who don't want to have to read through your article to get what they need.

Stolen Content

Myth: Pinterest allows stolen content and does nothing about it. Fact: Pinterest does not *allow* it (it's a bot issue). Every social media and search platform has had these types of growing pains in the past, and Pinterest is no exception. Pinterest has indicated that if you find your content stolen, send them an email with the content. I do know that Pinterest is exercising their legal rights and taking action against alleged offenders, but that's all I know at this point.

Buyable & Promoted Pins

There are differences between buyable pins and promoted pins. Buyable pins are pins that allow you to purchase right from the platform. Promoted pins are just advertisements on Pinterest, but you can promote a buyable pin!

There really are not any good statistics available on whether people do a ton of buying with buyable pins. We can always speculate based on the number of Pinterest users and typical conversion with any platform of ___%, but there's no real data on this available anywhere. Knowing the typical Pinterest user, we doubt many of them are using buyable pins, but I do have clients that have shopped via Pinterest, so it's always something to try out if you're able to do so.

Another question I get asked is whether promoting a brand new pin will cost more than letting it gain traction organically before taking out a promotion ad. It's all based on your targeting and use of keyboards. If you and a billion other people are targeting a keyword you'll definitely pay a lot more than if it's just a few hundred other people. When your pin does well as a promoted pin, you're going to pay less—this is why testing out your pins is so important. I highly recommend using promoted pins as part of your overall Pinterest strategy.

Other Questions

How can you get information directly from Pinterest? Pinterest hasn't really been open to sharing a ton of information with the blogging community over the years, so it often feels as though we have to poke and prod around to find it. But they have done a much better job of updating the Pinterest pinning community via their blog. Keep in mind that Pinterest built their platform for pinners and consumers, not content creators. So any updates and information that they choose to share with us is icing on the cake.

19 MANUAL PINNING VS. SCHEDULED PINNING: WHICH ONE GETS BETTER RESULTS?

Top category in the US is Art, Art Supplies & Hobbies.

N ow it's time to talk about something that is really important, especially for those of you just starting out with Pinterest marketing. I've read and researched lots of conversations and articles about manual pinning vs. scheduled pinning. What's important to remember that you need a system in place to be successful with Pinterest. Big bloggers, including me, have made mistakes along the way with marketing, and this thing about manual versus automated or scheduled pinning is a tough question. I know a lot about Pinterest and am happy to share some of my experiences and results personally as well as share what others have discovered.

If you're new to Pinterest marketing...

One thing I want you to really wrap your head around is finding a strategy that works for you that is efficient and impactful on Pinterest that boosts your page views without consuming your time. Pinning with intention is important. It's not fruitful to pin without a strategy in place if you're using Pinterest for gaining page views. Evaluate what you're spending your time on. Start with a balanced approach of pinning some of your pins and others' pins and evolve from there, while carefully looking at your results.

What Exactly is Manual Pinning?

Manual or "live" pinning is when you take a pin on your site, or another blogger's site, and use their social sharing buttons to share it. It's also the art of being on Pinterest and pinning your own content and re-pinning others' pins on a regular, routine basis.

Manual pinning also includes those scenarios where you upload an image to Pinterest directly without using software or a service, and add your description and URL to pin it to your board. Manual pinning occurs when you are actually on the Pinterest platform itself, whether through the app on your mobile phone, tablet, or on a computer.

What is Automated or Scheduled Pinning?

Automated or scheduled pinning is when you use a platform, like Tailwind or Buffer, for example, to add your pins to your Pinterest profile. The Pinterest scheduler slowly drips your pins to your designated Pinterest for you onto the board you want based on a schedule you have set. It is a simple way to make sure you pin a specific number of pins every single day.

So many schedulers, so little time.

Which automated pinning system is the best? What are the Pinterest scheduler options? Buffer and ViralTag also enable you to schedule pins. Hootsuite allows you to schedule but you have to own a Tailwind account for the connection. Tailwind is the most popular at the moment, but I believe that the BoardBooster team will be back in the next year with even better software. And it's only a matter of time before another company comes up with even better software than what is currently available, so be sure to follow my blog so you get the latest updates on new and emerging software available to you.

Pinterest has a list of approved partners that you can check out on their site to research which system is most ideal for your pinning and scheduling needs. An approved partner essentially means that Pinterest has given approval for them to use the Pinterest API (the key that allows them to share Pinterest content). Other systems can schedule, but they are not approved partners. So if you're using one of these alternative schedulers, it's important to understand that you're going against the terms and services for using Pinterest.

The Theory Behind Manual Pinning

When people start pinning manually, they sometimes get more traffic. Never assume, though, that the reason behind the uptick in traffic is solely due to your manual pinning methods. The real truth could be a combination of other reasons, such as a pin that suddenly gains traction or a phenomenal pin that is currently a hot topic or extremely relevant to your audience, pinning one pin to the right board, or capitalizing on trending Pinterest topics. There are so many variables and moving parts on Pinterest that it is nearly impossible to attribute the changes in traffic to just manual pinning.

In order to be absolutely sure that a particular Pinterest strategy has been successful for you, it requires measuring data before, during and after the strategy is implemented. Keep an eye of your statistics in your Pinterest Analytics area, and also look at your individual pin success from time to time.

In this day of automation, why would anyone want to do manual pinning?

Some people like to be in complete control of their pinning experience. They want to know when exactly a pin is going to post. They like to have knowledge of their pinning activities and which pins get more attention on various boards.

In addition, there seems to be a lot of skepticism floating around about using automated schedulers. Provided they are an approved provider, they are perfectly acceptable to use in the eyes of the Pinterest platform. Automation does not have to be an ugly word. Just because one person has had immense success with pinning manually should not discount the thousands of us that have had success using automation, as well. This is, unfortunately, a common occurrence with new people to Pinterest marketing. They hear one thing from one successful person and just go with it. Well, we learned the hard way this year in believing from one major person who claimed that BoardBooster was the best way to pin, didn't we. Board-Booster unfortunately was NOT the best way because it wasn't an approved partner and shut down. So even though you've read this book and have learned everything you need to know from me, I would hope that you would reach out to other pinners and get their opinions on what has worked for them, as well. I tend to take a conservative approach with Pinterest while still being considered a "power user" (account with consistently 100k+ views per month). Maybe you're comfortable with following my strategies and my methods. Maybe you want to try something different. It's completely up to you! I always like hearing from people who have read my books and discovering what THEY have discovered through their testing.

Now, the last important thing to remember that an account with a high number of page views (such as mine) does not necessarily mean that behind the scenes their conversion is successful. The true test of Pinterest marketing is to measure your two sets of data - your total page views and your total income. Are you making money? Page views mean nothing if you are not converting those numbers into sales. Before you start copying what someone else is doing, evaluate whether or not their methods would increase your revenue.

My personal experience in pinning on Pinterest from 2017-2018

I, like many others, used BoardBooster and saw great results from it back in 2017. Pinterest had only begun the process of requiring any apps to be API-compliant. BoardBooster at the time was our best friend, even though they were not an "approved" partner. In fact, many experts with big account activity on Pinterest, and I mean, 45k+ followers, used and recommended using BoardBooster. It worked for us. But then, sadly, in 2018 it shut down at the request of Pinterest because they had not received the API approval as a partner.

When many of us switched to manual pinning and stopped using BoardBooster from time to time, we noticed an increase in traffic. Several of my online friends and colleagues who are really into Pinterest had read about manual pinning getting better results than automated or scheduled pinning. So it was definitely worth a try.

Tracie used to use Boardbooster and noticed her traffic decreasing. She knew they were not an approved partner, but some "experts" that she had listened to swore it was the only way to use Pinterest and she followed along. Just like others, she had read that manual pinning was getting people more traffic and she stopped scheduling and started manually pinning. Admittedly, she hated it, because it tied her to her computer every day but thought that she had to continue because it was going to get good results.

After doing some manually pinning for a couple months without using a service, my traffic started to increase again. It was like I wasn't being "punished" by Pinterest anymore. It was incredibly time consuming, though. I did have a Tailwind account, too, but have never been too thrilled with the user experience, although for busy marketers like myself without a lot of time to pin a lot, Tailwind right now is probably your best option. I've tried every single app and pinning service out there. I'm back to 8 hours per month in scheduling and planning my content for Pinterest.

Like every other professional marketer using Pinterest, I've experienced my share of dips in traffic. Some forms of content are just more popular than others. But the goal really should be to focus on your boards that get the most amount of traffic and attention by other users and pinners, so you have steady traffic coming in and growth in your numbers. Once you have that under control you can then focus on your less-popular boards and work their content better. I think you'll find steady consistency and growth with using a scheduler. The downside is that for many bloggers, they can be cost-prohibitive, so try to plan for this cost in your budget allocation.

What is really more important than manual vs. automated pinning?

Keywords and images. Images that beautiful and vivid combined with specific keywords are even more important as they tie directly to the Pinterest algorithm. Manual vs. automated pinning doesn't effect the algorithm as much because the power of the smart feed focuses on images, keywords and the authority of your domain.

Don't base your decision on whether to go manual vs. scheduled/automated based on one person's experience. Try to weigh the opinion and experiences of several people that may or may not be in your same field of niche. Some people have better experiences with pinning manually than they do with schedulers. And vice versa.

You might be asking, well, what do YOU do? I use a scheduler, Tailwind, along with pinning manually throughout the day. I have time to spend doing sporadic pinning with little breaks in my day, and I still enjoy doing hashtag and keyword searches.

Be open to trying new things, especially if you're not getting the results you want. If you keep doing the same thing expecting different results, believe me, nothing is going to change. Try changing things up, checking your keywords, and switch to manual pinning every once in a while. You'll never know what could be unless you give it a try.

20 HOW TO WORK AND PIN AT HOME WITH KIDS

Recipes: There are more than 1.7 billion recipe pins.

L et's say you are busy. SUPER busy. With kids. Say no more, right? What is it like to work at home with kids or even do a full-time job during the day and come home to work on your blog at night while raising kids? Ha!

A lot of my readers are stay-at-home moms, raising babies and blogging, trying hard to bring income to the table and challenge themselves. It's hard to be productive when you have kids in the house and you're trying to get work done. Let's just be honest about that. Kids can be productivity ninja-slayers. You being the ninja. You're dead. They won.

Ah, but there is hope, my friend.

If you have kids who are five and under, this is a hard, super hard phase in your life the way it is. There are unpredictables impacting your blogging and pinning time left and right, just waiting to surface and bite your butt. Here are some things I recommend if you're battling both young ages and day jobs / other responsibilities. I've been there, and am currently STILL in this phase with three kids under the age of five. My other three are older, but all of them are currently (as of date of publication) under the age of 10.

Let me assure you, it does get better, but don't get upset when your well-intentioned plans don't pan out. Just roll with it and use special carved-out periods of time you know you can count on (theoretically) to get your pinning work done.

Work During Nap Time

I love nap time. Nap time means "mommy's work time". You're going to have to battle with the urge to take a nap yourself (guilty) but if you can muster up the energy, this is going to be a power hour for you to get some work done. Hint on battling urges to nap right along with your babies - take a "creative refresh" shower - just a 10 minute shower to dust yourself off and feel better, and more energized. You'll be ready to work again.

Work in the Evenings

Try doing your pinning in the evenings, doing some for yourself to fill your creative well for the next day or following week, and a lot for your blog and followers. Evenings on Pinterest are super hot anyway, so you'll see a lot of new stuff coming out. The kids are also winding down or in bed, and it's a great time to work silently on something that doesn't require a lot of brain power. I love winding down with Pinterest in the evening, and so does my husband. It's our pillow talk for projects and dreams.

My husband does his pinning for Mancave Mayhem (pinterest.com/mancavemayhem) in the morning and in the evening. Just by listening to me, and asking questions, he has built an account on Pinterest from zero to over 200k in just over a month. Then, he worked on publishing his first book on Amazon a home improvement planner. And he sold 4 copies without any ad spend or heavy broadcasting. I think I may have mentioned it twice on social media so he was really excited. And with the kids around, it's hard for him, too, to focus on pinning during the day because he'd rather be helping with schoolwork and taking them out to play sports.

Working Away from Home

Any time I'm gearing up for a newsletter or a new product idea, I go work in a coffee shop. It's quiet time away from the kids and chaos, and it really helps you map out each step of what needs to be done, because not every single project or product is going to be the same.

Try working away from your comfort zone in your house and get productive in a coffee shop, library or somewhere else that allows you to set up shop, sip hot or chilled cozy drinks and get your work done. You'll feel refreshed and productive by the time you get home.

Consider Service Professionals for Help Around the House

There was a point in my blogging career where I was amping up so much that I couldn't bear to even think about doing laundry and vacuuming. I hired a maid to come every week to come out and help with that. The benefit far outweighed the cost, and I was able to get my work accomplished, which felt really good. And I had a clean house. Totally worth it.

SO USING these methods WILL help you get your work done. I can speak to this as a mom of six boys with every day varying and no real schedule. Because, well, boys. It does get better with time and training your kids to know that "hey, I'm working, can you show me your pretty drawing later?" And then, give them all the attention in the world when you're done.

21 MY VERY KERRIE TIPS

Shopping: Every day nearly 2M people pin product rich pins.

L et's go through my bottom-line tips for Pinterest because you've read into enough detail that it's actually time to start implementing everything.

Use Pinterest's verification tool to claim and confirm your website address.

The verification tool allows Pinterest to see that you in fact own the website you are linking to the account. In addition, it provides in-depth detail on how your pins from your website are performing along with the traffic you're receiving.

Be sure to enable Rich Pins.

Rich Pins are the way to go, and there are several reasons. The wonderful part about Rich Pins is that their metadata can be updated with any update you make to a page description. Prior to Rich Pins, pins on Pinterest would often include outdated information, such as pricing, page description, and so on. Now, with the newest updates in place from their platform given all the changes in the past years, if you change the price on a product, every single Rich Pin of that item on Pinterest will automatically update, making it easy to keep customers satisfied and up-to-date with the most recent information.

Use a high-resolution, professional photo of yourself or your business logo for your profile picture.

While it's not important to hire a photographer to do a photo shoot of yourself and your business office, it is important to use a photo that is well-lit, bright and of high-resolution. A high-resolution business logo for more business-related Pinterest profiles will work nicely, as well.

Find good people to follow.

This is also a good way to gain followers, as well, even though Pinterest really isn't a follow-for-follow kind of platform. The best way to find good people or boards to follow is to find your favorite entrepreneurs on Pinterest and click on who they are following. Follow the people or boards you find most applicable to your platform and you'll probably gain some followers back, too.

Find the content your readers are already pinning.

Visit pinterest.com/source/yoursite.com to see the content your readers are already pinning.

Just be you. Don't copy everyone else.

There are a ton of #girlboss, #ladyboss, #momboss, and #girlbosses out there who talk about making money online and typically use all the same colors and fonts. Please do not feel pressured to copy into this theme just because you perceive them as successful. Be your own person. You'll note that there are a ton of pink-oriented pins on Pinterest. Notice that my profile adopts the soft blue and ocean & relaxation feel. It's what works for me, and is my signature style. So find what your brand colors are and stick to YOUR brand.

Track your analytics from the start.

What you'll find is that Pinterest provides great analytics, but only for the past 30 days. By using a spreadsheet, you can easily keep track of your success over time.

The "best time" to pin is somewhat irrelevant.

Pinterest's Smart Feed determines when and where your pins are shown, and this is why it's so important to put out your very best pins. Pin schedulers like Buffer and Tailwind can help you maintain consistency in pinning, but try not to get too wrapped up in the concept of the "best" time to pin.

Full descriptions in your pins is best.

You're allotted about 500 characters for your pin's description, so try to ensure you're using all of the available space given to you. Pinners will only see a short preview, so be sure to wow them with the first sentence, followed with some hashtags. Don't worry - the Smart Feed and search engine will read your whole description; not just your preview.

Keep the number of lifestyle boards in check.

You don't need to create a ton of lifestyle boards or follow a ton of them, either. Everything in moderation. If you're not blogging about lifestyle options and solutions, then lifestyle may not exactly be relevant to your audience, even though it seems they may be popular. The goal is to have a dedicated following of people who love seeing and reading about your pins, and re-pinning them. It's better to have relevancy and a high-performing niche than it is to have lifestyle boards that are popular.

Find high-quality content.

Always keep the good stuff coming from your blog and website. If you want to drive traffic back to your website, you have to deliver good material. And, you're only going to want to follow people you can actually re-pin content from. It's good to keep a notebook of search keywords and hashtags to continually check for new content and new bloggers.

Use secret boards to hide stuff you don't want your readers to see or that may be irrelevant to your audience.

Just because you may not see recipes on my boards doesn't mean I don't have recipes stored on my Pinterest account. I don't talk about recipes and food on my main blog, so I keep recipes for my family to try and make in a secret board so my viewers don't see it. They probably don't need to see my long list of charcuterie boards and cupcake recipes. Keeping your boards clean and free of irrelevant content makes it super easy to clean up your boards in the future. Secret boards are also perfect for storing upcoming project ideas or blog post ideas that you don't want people to know about yet.

Only pin on-brand content.

Pinterest does in fact limit the total number of pins you can share over time per account, and this is where the concept of quality over quantity comes into play. When we talk about on-brand content, we mean that only content relevant to our audience and subject matter should be pinned. You can even take it a step further and brand your boards with a consistent color scheme and style, and only pin similar pins with the same colors, look, and feel.

Use the notifications alert to identify pinning ideas Pinterest is showing you.

When Pinterest is alerting you of things and pins that are popular or that you may be interested, take that opportunity and start pinning. Rumor has it that Pinterest will "elevate" your account and show more of your pins if you pin material that they have identified as applicable to you. This can also help you save time in identifying what to pin next.

Make use of seasonal content if it's applicable.

If your blog or website discusses seasonal content like Easter, 4th of July, Halloween, Thanksgiving, and Christmas, then you'll want to start pinning your material two months in advance to the actual holiday date. You'll see an increase in your analytics and stats as a result by timing seasonal content correctly. Remember - Pinterest helps pinners determine what they want to try and buy next, especially in the gift-giving seasons.

The most important board - your board.

The first board people see on your profile should be a board reserved exclusively for your own content. This board should also be added to your showcase (the rotating feature setting where you can feature five of your boards). You'll want to post your own content in your other boards, as well, but it's important to have your first board highlighting all of your website and blog content.

Get more followers by being attractive.

Having an attractive and cohesive look to your Pinterest profile will help you gain followers quickly and serve you well long-term. Your pins should be tall, pretty (whatever that means to you), easy to read, and as much as possible, provide value to your audience.

Test for pin size and screen size.

The standard pin size is 764x1104 (or thereabouts), but you'll want to make sure your pins look good on mobile devices, tablets, as well as your website.

#PinterestGoals - multi-dimensional pins

One of your goals with using Pinterest is going to be a bit of a design and theme challenge. Try using pins that blend well but also multiple colors and textures that compliment your brand well. Try not to stick to just one color.

Use less-popular stock photos.

It's easy to get caught up with using photos that are free and available on Unsplash.com and other free photo stock sites. There are a ton of other photo sites I mentioned earlier that will give your brand some pop if you need a 3rd party supplier of photo stock and are unable to do your own.

Create impressive and attractive board cover photos.

You don't necessarily need to create pins just for your board covers unless you really want to. You can take your best-designed and most popular pin and use that for your board cover, as well. Using a similar color or theme for each board cover is a must here.

Make it easy for people to pin from your site

Plugins, if a Pinterest feature doesn't come with your site's theme design, will help you ensure your site is pinnable. Test it from different devices and ensure your plugin or Pinterest pinning feature is working correctly.

Optimize and review your content often.

It's always a good idea to go back (in time) and look at some of your older pins that are not performing as well and perhaps update your content along with the pin image. Freshen up the pin on the page with something new and even more appealing. It may just do the trick.

Add links to your Pinterest profile on your website.

Let people know you're active on Pinterest. Encourage them to follow you whenever it's appropriate, and include your links on your site in all the right places - header, sidebar, footer, and within each blog post (you can use a content-at-bottom feature here).

Use this code to hide Pinterest images.

<div   style="display: none;">YOUR   IMAGE HERE</div>

This code hides Pinterest images where it may not be ideal to have them. It still allows people to pin your content, but will not show the pin image on the page.

Install a social media sharing plugin.

A sharing bar or a social media sharing plugin helps people know how many times your article or page has been shared. By nature, people tend to share popular things.

Make sure all your images have Pinterest-friendly ALT text.

This will help enhance your overall SEO and boost your pin's ability to be searched. When I started focusing on the file names and ALT text of my images on my own site, I found my Pinterest game improved a great deal.

Use the Pinterest widget builder.

The widget builder is easy to install and can be prominently displayed on your website, making it easy for people to see what you pin and to re-pin some of yours from your own collections, boards, and profile. The widget builder can be used to display certain boards (or your whole account) on sites other than Pinterest. If it works in your post, you could create a widget for one of your related boards. If you find yourself, for example, referencing a specific collection, you could implement a Pinterest board to share in a blog post. This could even work if you have a collection of books or bloggers you recommend.

Try asking your readers to "Try It!" on Pinterest at the end of your blog post.

When you combine the power of re-pins along with "Tried It" adds to your pins, you're playing a winning game. Ask, at the end of each blog post, to have your audience mark their pins with "tried it!". This plays well for the Pinterest Smart Feed.

Organize your boards by importance, and then topic.

Google has demonstrated to the Pinterest crowd that boards listed by importance matters. So place your boards with keywords specific to your niche at the top of your Pinterest profile in order of importance.

Combine niche keywords along with personality in your Pinterest profile bio.

The market is flooded with creators, coaches and entrepreneurial buzz words. Try to be a little "extra" niche-marketed by combining your standard niche keywords along with some added pizazz in your bio. This may gain you a few extra sets of eyes on your profile.

Have multiple boards for "umbrella" boards, but then get specific with keywords.

It makes sense to pin the same pin to multiple boards. You don't have to just pin to one board. For example, blogging and social media are often intertwining. So I have a blogging board, but I also have a social media tips. I can easily pin the same pin in both boards. Don't limit one pin to one board. Re-pin a piece of content to as many boards that make sense.

Name your boards according to function - don't be cute.

Remember - Pinterest is a search engine. If you get too specific or cute with your naming conventions, people will NOT find your pins. For example: Thanksgiving Recipes vs. November Splendor - Things to Try. Which are people more likely to search for? Thanksgiving Recipes. I don't recall the last time I used the term "splendor" to search for anything. At all. So keep things search-friendly with your boards. Avoid using spaces and special characters.

Use the Pinterest Search Bar.

Pinterest's search bar is going to be one of your best friends. If you don't know which keywords to use, use the search bar and start typing in something similar to what you think you would use. Pinterest, just like Amazon and Google, will give you suggestions.

Be sure to know what dictates how well your content performs.

The time you pin doesn't matter. Deleting older, non-performing pins doesn't matter. What DOES matter is the quality of your real estate - your domain, your pin quality (such as the number of pins vs. re-pins you have), relevance of your pins to your subject matter, and your quality as a Pinterest pinner—not spamming, not violating DMCA laws, and pinning high-quality content regularly.

Long-tail keywords are best in blog posts.

Make sure your blog posts are not "thin". Longer, more wordier and richer blog posts rich with content are better found and discovered on both Pinterest and Google.

The Smart Feed is your friend.

The smart feed pulls pins from three main sources—re-pins from people you follow, pins related to the kind of content you pin, and pins that may be related to the content you tend to click on or search for (or your interests). This is also why you don't want to follow just anyone.

Try not to use "other" for your board classification.

Again, this is a search engine and the Pinterest algorithm will show people pins based on interests. So if they're interested in "geek" things and you have geek as your board category instead of "other", you'll show up.

Join Group Boards!

Group boards are intended to be a "plus" to your normal pinning strategy. If you want ways to expand your reach, joining group boards is just one way. Make sure the group board is relevant and high-performing before you join. If you discover that it's just not for you, no worries. They will not receive an alert that you left the group.

Pin your pins to multiple boards throughout the day.

This is the best way to keep your new content alive and well on Pinterest and to get it moving. Don't just pin to the same board over and over. Use multiple boards and spread the same pin over multiple boards throughout the day. You'll have the best impact that way. Don't do the one-and-done thing. (Pinning to one board, with one pin, and nothing else).

Be sure to connect with the brands you talk about in your pin.

Hidden opportunities are waiting for you! You never know when a brand will pick up your pinned content as a promotional piece for their next promotional fleet or better yet, they might pin your pin and promote it on their mega-huge Pinterest profile.

Join targeted Tailwind Tribes.

Getting your pins in front of relevant Tailwind tribe members just escalates the push of your pins. Instead of having to wait for your pin to be discovered, tribes makes it possible for your pin to be seen instantly by everyone in the tribe.

Create your own Group Board when you've mastered everything else.

Running a group board is not for the faint-of-heart. A successful group board requires managing and oversight. Only take this on when you feel as though your numbers are excellent, you're making money, and have the time to commit to this. Don't accept just anyone into your group. Be targeted and selective. Invite collaborators that you know would do a great job and not spam their content all over your group board.

Tag other bloggers.

Be sure to tag other bloggers if you've given them some shining light on your posts and pins. It's how we work together as a great community! They'll most likely share your pin which will result in re-shares and re-pins, for sure.

45. Concentrate on boosting your engagement rate, NOT your follower count.

The Smart Feed wants pins that are getting clicks and repins. Pinterest doesn't care if you have a million followers if they're ghosts that never click on or repin your content.

46. Forget about opt-ins for a minute, and put a call-to-action at the bottom of your post, asking your reader to pin your content.

Pinterest is going NOWHERE anytime soon; this is not a Snapchat, Instagram, or Vine situation. If you're posting a recipe or DIY, ask your readers to click the "Try It!" button on Pinterest.

Don't get frustrated.

Pinterest requires patience. And lots of time. It will take time for your account to start taking off. If you stop, you'll lose all that building momentum. When you're first starting out, give it 2-3 months to catch up to your efforts before you try something different. Pinterest WILL update your monthly viewer count on a weekly basis. It updates your analytics account nightly. So give a big strategy some time to take flight before you throw in the towel. And remember —professional pinners like myself are just an email away if you need a second pair of eyes on your strategy.

Refresh your content.

A fresh image can do wonders for older content. Don't be afraid to make a new pin for older content. Don't be afraid to freshen up an older blog post with updated, even-more-relevant information. Revive everything you possibly can to get the conversions going.

Use the 30-day trial on Tailwind.

If you're not sure about using paid software for your Pinterest efforts, give it a try. You can get a 30-day trial absolutely free and see if it's helping. But to be honest, with anything, it's going to take some time. So before you get rolling with that new Tailwind account, make sure you don't waste days by not having your "stuff" together.

Use Tailwind to check for missing items on your Pinterest account.

Tailwind has a feature on the Suggestions pane which will tell you if you're missing anything like board descriptions, pin suggestions, etc. Make sure you're going in on a regular basis and re-pinning your older content until you can use the looping feature.

Constantly improve your content (writing, headlines, branding, etc).

Never settle. Keep pushing for improvements and make branding, writing, and signup improvements to your site. Check every single article to see how you can make improvements and get people to convert to a sale. Every single post and page serves as an opportunity.

Revise your Pinterest strategy from time to time.

Just because something works for others, does not exactly mean it will work perfectly for you. It's essential to change up your strategy every once in a while if your Pinterest game isn't quite the winning one. If efficiency is your main problem, try using the "save as draft" feature on Tailwind. It'll help you rack up a ton of pins to eventually schedule, and then you may not have to work so hard or long in scheduling. If getting your pins to "go viral" is the problem, try joining or applying to some group boards. Doing the same thing while expecting different results will get you nowhere.

Make friends with other bloggers.

There are Facebook groups dedicated to online marketers just like you. Tap into the groups on Facebook and other forums. Just make sure that the group activity is focused on helping you stay on-brand.

Fresh ideas are best.

I can't tell you how many pins there are about "How to Start a Blog". Move beyond that and blog and pin something much more interesting. Change up your headline. Make it a pin they absolutely have to read. Don't be generic - stay fresh with your ideas.

Try promoting a pin.

Once you're good and comfortable with the art of pinning on Pinterest, try your hand at promoting a pin. Make sure that you use the audience feature and keywords to target the right people. Generally, promotions on Pinterest are inexpensive. Some of my ads have been $.01 per engagement. So there is hope for inexpensive advertising if you try things out and experiment!

Use the boards list feature in Tailwind for ultimate efficiency.

Because efficiency is a must when working on Pinterest, it's a good idea to decrease the amount of repetitive tasks involved with pinning by using the boards list feature on Tailwind. This way you can group the boards together and classify your pins based on your lists, instead of having to pin directly to each one separately.

Stay classy. Don't spam.

It's incredibly easy to get caught up with pinning all the things from your blog and wanting to be seen. The thing with that is it's incredibly self-serving instead of an act based on sharing. Pinterest, while being a search engine, still is a community based on sharing and re-pinning. If you're only sharing your materials and no one else's... the likelihood that people will want to share your pins only decreases.

Hundreds of pins per day is unnecessary at first.

If you really want to pin 100 or more pins per day by all means do that, but it's not necessary, especially when you're first starting out. Start with 20-30 per day, work your way up to 60-70 per day, and then find your groove as close to 100 as possible. But remember - quality or quantity. Don't just pin pins to make a quota.

Try to pin organically when you have time.

Pinterest still loves organic pinning. We live and operate in a world of automation, but Pinterest does "award" for organic pinning activity. If you're standing in line somewhere, pin away. If you need a break from writing, pin a little bit and then go on with your activity.

Don't bother with deleting low-performing pins.

You never know when a pin will take off. Maybe the subject matter just isn't popular yet. Maybe you just need to adjust the keywords or send it to your tribes, or even try some new images or a headline. Deleting pins is simply a waste of time unless you've determined that it no longer has a place on your boards.

Focus on delivering value.

Delivering value does not mean giving away your products or services for free. It means providing your very best and helping others while still leaving an income opportunity open.

Pin content you wish you had known years ago.

Are there things you wish you had known about your niche topic years or even a year ago? Pin that content. It'll help someone else, and you'll probably gain a lot of follower trust as a result.

To pin from Facebook groups or not?

Some will claim that participating in pin-for-pin groups on Facebook or niche groups is empty engagement. However, I've found that in some instances, people have discovered my content and continue to follow me as a result of pin-for-pin group activity.

Don't delete boards. Make them secret.

When and if you delete a board on Pinterest, you lose the followers that once followed that board. So instead of deleting the board, simply make it secret.

For more reading, try the Pinterest Engineering Blog.

This is a blog available on Medium which may help give you more insight into Pinterest. It's worth reading and extremely valuable.

Remember - Pinterest is a search engine. It's not social media.

The premise of Pinterest and what drives it is not the concept of being social. Focus on your keywords, offering valuable content to gain trust and re-pins, and working your group boards. The goal is to remain search-friendly and to be found online so you can build your email list and make sales.

Pinterest vs. Social Media

It's not surprising to me when I hear about people giving up on Pinterest or that Pinterest isn't working "fast enough" like social media may. Social media like Instagram, Facebook, and Twitter may give the impression or results of a winning strategy, and sure, they have their good points. But unless you are willing to pay a great deal of money and continually throw money at these platforms, your reach will always be a bit more limited than what you could reach with Pinterest.

In addition, remember that a pin on Pinterest will net you far more results longer (in years) than a social media post that has a life-span of about 24-48 hours, if even that. Posts come and go. Pins last years. So with Pinterest, it's easy to feel like you are banging your head against a brick wall if you're not seeing results instantly. Stay patient.

I'm going to give you some things to check just to ensure that you're getting everything right, or need a refresher from an objective perspective.

• Check your image sizes. Make sure your pin images aren't exceeding 1260 pixels in length, and that you're using a pin size ratio of 6:9.

• Don't let your pins get too long, too cluttered, or too filled with text.

• Do your pins get to the point and pique their curiosity? You want them to not just save but also click through.

• Are you doing pin testing correctly? Use the same images for both pins, but different keywords and hashtags. Then, swap out and use a different image. Use more of what performs better.

• Get a professional blogger's feedback, even if that means paying money for their time and swallowing your pride. This is something that could be as easy as a small issue you're just not seeing. Like a font style, for example.

• Make sure you're not keyword stuffing and keep your pin descriptions natural.

• Don't use keywords that are not relevant with the hopes that people will find you. You'll annoy them instead, and look like you don't know what you're doing to the rest of the Pinterest community. Pinterest is all about relevance so don't put your account in jeopardy.

• Use rich keyword phrases as opposed to just one-word keywords.

• Leverage your audience by reminding your audience weekly to follow you on Pinterest.

• Remind people on your blog to save things for later.

• Install share buttons on your site and make sure they're working.

• Check to make sure your mobile website version is responsive and provides a good pinning experience.

• Share your boards on your blog posts.

• Cross-promote your Pinterest boards and account on your social media platforms.

22 BUSINESS TIPS

50% have made a purchase after seeing a promoted pin.

In this chapter we're going to be talking about increasing sales by converting Pinterest traffic to get your products and services selling consistently.

Many bloggers I've talked to online are engaging in "passive selling", which means they're just making money off of ads when Pinterest users come to their site. In this chapter, I want to give you some advice on how to strategically sell on your site

Sales Coaching and Communication

My tendency is to work with entrepreneurs to teach them how to sell in an authentic way so that they're able to build strong relationships with the communities they've built or are trying to build, and ultimately make more sales. I'm more of a sales coach who has studied how people communicate and receive information. Knowing how you're showing up in the world on Pinterest and how other people are showing up on your site allows you to be more flexible in your sales skills and communication behavior. Communication skills are critical, because sales really boil down to the level of relationship and trust you have with your audience.

Pinterest traffic can really fluctuate. Sometimes we have roaring months of endless traffic and triple our page views, sometimes, even the biggest Pinterest power users have down months where we trickle down to our consistent level of traffic that has become the "norm". When people visit your site from a pin, they came for a purpose and will leave fairly quickly. You only have a small window of time to capture them. Scheduling your pins, creating beautiful images and having an intriguing post headline, and having SEO-optimized pin descriptions are all wonderful and important things to do, but the real magic happens when they get to your site. It's that moment where you'll need to try to convert them.

4 Important Tips for Converting Pinterest Traffic into Sales

Tip 1: Tailor Your Language

When you are writing—whether that's content for your website, a newsletter, or emails – we tend to write from our own perspective. I'm even guilty of this from time to time. It makes sense to us to write in the first person point of view because we think from our perspective. However, your readers are interested in their own perspective, their needs, and their point of view. As you are writing content and trying to make your products and services sell, it's important to remember that the world does not revolve around you. It can be counterproductive to write in the first person when you're trying to draw readers to you.

I recommend writing your sentences using the "you" (second person) perspective instead of the "I" (first person) perspective. Your readers aren't coming to your site to hear all about you. When you change the language, it really draws them in. You want to make sure your message is about the reader and that it feels personal.

Changing the language and point of view can take a little extra effort if you're not used to writing that way, and perhaps maybe some extra thought, but the result is closing more sales, and creating much stronger relationships with your community. Answer their biggest challenge points and use your testimonials sparingly. Don't be afraid to share what other people are saying about you, but at the same time, don't overdo it. I've seen way too many instances of testimonial and review overkill where it almost seems "made up". Try to get three testimonials together to use in your sales efforts.

Tip 2: List Your Prices

There is nothing more annoying to people who visit your site to have to email you to find out what your prices are. It's an added step they really shouldn't have to do to get basic information. This advice runs counter to what many sales experts recommend, and I know that at a lot of car sales places they have "email for pricing" on their inventory, but hear me out on this.

Selling is really about the other person. It's not about you. It's about the customer. Make it easy for your clients to work with you, and you can do this by including your prices on your website. If you can't quote one price, at least provide a price range. You are there to be helpful and provide information. Not make it harder for them to get information.

I'm a firm believer that if people go to your site and don't see pricing, they aren't going to pick up the phone and call you or even email you (mainly because it makes them feel uncomfortable). Some people will assume that your prices are so high they won't be able to afford your services and not bother emailing or calling.

You've set your prices for a reason and know how long it takes to either create something or the work involved with working with someone. Only you know the quality and value of what you're offering. You need to be okay with sharing that openly and be proud and confident with what you charge. People can then choose to move forward with you if they like your work and products, or can quickly move on to someone cheaper if they can't afford your services/products.

Tip 3: Look for Ways to Say Yes Even from Your Freebie

As a graphic designer, I get a lot of requests from people to make changes to some of my content upgrades to suit their personal needs. Everything from changing the fonts to colors, to arranging the layout. At first, I was like, "it's a FREEBIE"—take it for what it is. Because, I don't have time to work for free.

But then I got smart (after being fairly annoyed with the requests). I started saying "Sure, no problem. It'll cost ____ to make those changes." And some of the people who messaged me were willing to pay, and of course, some were not.

Figure out how you can make money from your free product. Make sure you're charging for your talent, hard work, and expertise. People are paying you for your unique talents.

Tip 4: ROO – Return On Opportunity

You've probably heard the term ROI, or return on investment. I feel return on opportunity, or ROO, is just as important as ROI. If you are driving people to your site, they may not buy the first time they visit because they're just getting to know you, but you do want to stay in their inbox or have them subscribe to you. Get their attention.

This is where you'll want to create an irresistible freebie or offer that prompts them to join your email list. Stay engaged with these people through a sales funnel that is carefully crafted and written specifically related to what you offer and what the freebie is related to, because the return on opportunity comes down to the convincing strategy—whether or not you've provided them with value, good pricing, and a quality product/service.

Remember this: everyone has a limited number of times that they'll say no to something before finally saying yes if your offer is compelling enough and matches their three requirements of value, price, and quality.

Your focus needs to be on building trust with your audience and web visitors and draw them in so you can see that return on opportunity in the future. If someone decides to grab my free stock photos or a sample of my writing planner, and then a year later comes back to see if I have any new planner designs or stock photos, I've given them a return on opportunity.

We all want to experience an immediate response to our pins and get sales right away. It's easy to get discouraged and impatient when it doesn't happen. Give it some time. It's a long hard road to become an overnight success; one that takes time and a lot of A/B testing. If you're consistently putting good content out, and you're making it easy for people to work with you, you will start attracting people who will say yes to you every single time. This is just good strategy over tactics. It's important not to forget about the value of return on opportunity and how important that will be given a bit of time. Your efforts you put forth today can lead to sales years down the line, even if you feel like your efforts are a failure in the present due to lack of instant results.

Action Steps

I know making these changes are going to take some time. Go through your blog and take action on two of the four steps right away just to make some positive changes. Then come back after you've mastered those two steps and work on the other two.

23 PINNING CHECKLIST

Promoted pins are re-pinned an average of 11 times per advertisement.

L et's say you're just getting started with Pinterest and pinning. What are the most crucial steps before you start pinning anything and everything from your blog and from other boards?

There's a bit of a little checklist that goes into all of this pinning strategy. Most of what I recommend here applies mostly to bloggers and content creators. But there are a fair share of Shopify, Etsy, Artsy, WooCommerce, BigCommerce, and other storefront users that need to know what to do, as well, so be sure that you apply what I recommend here for your own situation. However, a lot of my tips for optimizing your website and online store are applicable to everyone on Pinterest, so just a heads up there.

For this project, let's make sure that your Pinterest boards are all cleaned up and optimized for keywords, you have your branded board covers done, and you have your content planned out. You'll want to make sure you have a clean start before you commence your pinning strategy.

Pre-Pinning To-Do List

1. For all images you upload into your site, ensure that the alt-text or Pinterest description is completed. You may have several images uploaded into a post or a page, and you never know what a user may choose to pin, so having all images appropriated tagged, described and filled with the alt-text is imperative. The alt-text should include 1-2 sentences to describe what the pinned article or page is about, written with keywords scattered throughout, in a natural conversational tone.

2. Add 5-6 hashtags to your description in the pin. Use hashtags that match the content keywords within your sentences, as well as one branded hashtag. For example, mine is #verykerrie, and for the majority of my pins, you'll see my hashtags there.

3. Many themes, especially newer ones, have custom Pin-It buttons that will embed themselves on your images, prompting your reader to pin your images for later reading, or to save for later reference. There are many plugins that you can choose from. My recommendation is to try one at a time and see which one converts the best for your particular site.

4. Lastly, it's wise to add a link or widget to your post for your reader to follow you on Pinterest. I do this often, leaving an example board that is related to my post or page, so they're equipped with some ideas that are curated from other blogs, too. My account grows by over 100 new followers on average now (I spent about two years hovering at 3000-4000 before I started really growing). Encourage your readers to pin your page for future reference. The best way to do this is to use a "below content" or "after post" widget so that you don't have to manually do this with each and every single post or page. Top-rated themes will have this area in the design of the theme automatically.

Use the widget builder tool on Pinterest and give your readers the option to follow your whole profile (recommend having this in your sidebar widget), a board, a custom board size, a banner, etc. Offer other related boards that they might be interested in.

Also, ask people to comment on your pin or prompt them with a "Tried This?" statement.

Now, let's talk about board relevancy. Your board relevancy is the board most closely associated with what you do and what you offer your readers. Pay extra close attention to this board with the use of keywords so that you send Pinterest the right signals about what you pin about, and the types of keywords that are most relevant to your account.

That's it! Remember, a pin lasts for a very long time. It's not like a social media post that has a lifespan of about 24 hours. Taking the time to pin things correctly and accurately will give you much more benefit than pinning without a winning strategy.

24 USING HASHTAGS ON PINTEREST

Articles: More than 14 million articles are pinned each day.

What's the rule about hashtags - how many can or should you use?

You can use up to 20 hashtags on a pin, but my recommendation is to use as many *relevant* hashtags as you can that describe your pin. You only have 500 characters as a limit in your Pinterest description, so you can't get too crazy with hashtags. What I'd recommend is develop a series of hashtag lists that are relevant for more of your posts, and store them in a text file for future use for whenever you're doing a pinning spree.

Just like you would on Instagram, always put hashtags at the end of the pin description. Users are accustomed (like on Instagram, LinkedIn, etc.) to reading the description and then seeing the hashtags at the end. Your description should be easy to read.

I also recommend using a branded hashtag (for me it's #verykerrie at the beginning of your hashtag list so that people can click on it and see all of the pins you've posted on Pinterest. It's a great way to get more exposure and get people over to your blog.

You can use hashtags in board names as well. Putting hashtags in board names has been shown to boost the performance of those boards in searches. The best thing to do is some testing, so go ahead and test out hashtags using one relevant hashtag at the end of your board name!

How specific do hashtags need to be?

Use a combination of broad and specific hashtags. You don't want to be so obtuse that no one actually searches for that hashtag. The broader hashtags will help you show up in the search feed and will show up chronologically. Using more specific hashtags will help you show up when someone searches for something specific. For example, *website design* could serve as a broader hashtag while *feminine wordpress themes* could be used as a more fine-tuned hashtag.

You can use Pinterest to discover what keywords and keyword phrases people search for to find your posts and use those keywords as hashtags by starting to type in a search phrase, and you'll see a whole submenu of keyword ideas available to you.

What about old pins and posts - should those be updated with hashtags?

You don't need to go back to every single pin and post unless it is sending you traffic. Instead, I would recommend going back into the blog posts and update the pin description to add some relevant hashtags there, but only with pins/blog posts that are getting traffic or have seasonal relevance for your readers. Have a strategy behind why you're updating - don't go and make this a huge project that could be unnecessary without a revenue strategy behind it.

What are the statistics for each hashtag - are they available like they are on Instagram?

Remember that Pinterest is completely different than Instagram, and it's not a form of social media. Pinterest will always decide on various factors whether to show your pin. Quality image, description of the blog that the pin is linked to, board relevance, etc. So they're going to match the content the user is looking for based on those factors. So while Pinterest may show you results for a hashtag, they will not be showing it in the same fashion or style as you would see on Instagram. What works for one platform may work differently for another.

Are Pinterest users actually clicking on the hashtags or are they just being found through search?

Users find hashtags through their search process. By positioning and choosing your hashtags carefully (remember, broad and specific), you'll send strong signals to Pinterest about your content.

Are pins with hashtags more likely to be stolen by scammers?

This is a tough one. Any pin has the likelihood of being lifted or stolen by an unscrupulous blogger that will redirect the traffic from the content shown on your pin to their site. My recommendation is not to worry about whether or not your content will be stolen by scammers more so if you use hashtags. Think more about what will happen to your content if you don't use hashtags. You will not be seen as much as you potentially could.

What if someone clicks on my hashtag and it sends them away from my pin?

Pinterest is all about discovery and being interested in specific things. You'll have that happen, but you'll also be on the receiving end of that behavior, as well. So there's going to be balance "in the force" with people clicking on hashtags and being directed elsewhere and also to your content. Primary focus here is to serve your audience, and give them content that is helpful.

Remember, when you see something new on social media, invest the time to learn about it so you're informed about potential opportunities that will play well with your current strategy. How will new changes in social media complement your Pinterest strategy? Are there time savers to be discovered? Test and analyze and figure out what strategy works for you, including your use of hashtags. See what happens. There is no defined "rule" on how to do Pinterest marketing. There are proven facts, guidelines, rules, and better strategies than others, but you won't learn new things if you sit around and wait for other people to come to tell you about them, if you don't try them out yourself.

25 HOW TO UPLOAD VIDEOS TO PINTEREST

High-income and educated US households are twice as likely to use Pinterest as low-income and less educated US households.

O ne of the new developments for Pinterest has been the ability to upload videos, in addition to pin images. There are a few things you'll need to know administratively in order to do this, though. So if you're into video or have thought about it, this is what you need to do.

You will need a Pinterest business account, so make sure you've converted your regular user account over to a business one as regular personal accounts will not have this option available. In addition, according to Pinterest, "only advertisers with a valid billing profile can upload a video on ads.pinterest.com or pinterest.com". While you don't have to promote it or spend money using your billing profile, having a billing account set up is how you will gain access to the video uploading option.

First, make sure the following specs are in place:

- File type: MP4 or MOV
- Resolution: Min 240p
- Max size: 2GB, or less; 30 min, or less
- Aspect ratio: Square (1:1); Vertical (9:16)
- Frame rate: Minimum 25fps

What kinds of videos do well on Pinterest? Food videos, crafts, DIY, how-tos and product features like the short and sweet style we often see on Facebook are the best kinds. Something that is easy for the user or reader to learn and implement, and inspires something new in their life. Inspirational, clever, and fun! Think about how your newly uploaded video can inspire your audience to take action and bring forth their creativity.

Step 1: Click on the '+' sign in the upper left of the screen to "upload a video".

Step 2: The next screen will pop up for you to upload your video, and you'll be provided with specifications on the upload. Upload a square version of the video. (1:1) Note that it could take a while for the video to upload.

Step 3: Capture the thumbnail shots you want while it's uploading or choose a custom thumbnail. Choose from the thumbnail options below the video.

Step 4: Add your description, hashtags, and website URL.

Step 5: Pick a board for your video.

Step 6: Wait for it to upload. It will say it's creating your promoted video, however, your video is not a promoted pin, so don't worry, you're not going to be promoting it through your billing account.

Step 7: Share the video with your people! Grab the pin link and share on other social channels or your email list.

That's it! Now you know how to upload videos to Pinterest so you can provide a wide variety of pin options for your audience to pin and learn from. This is just too easy, right?!

26 HOW TO CREATE A PINTEREST MARKETING PLAN

85 percent of women users use Pinterest to plan "life moments"

Next I'm going to show you how create a Pinterest marketing plan to get more clicks, subscribers, and sales. This is something that ANY blogger, regardless of niche, will be able to do. Whether you're an author, Etsy seller, sell a service - no matter what - you'll be able to create a Pinterest marketing plan.

Creating Your Plan

How is a busy blogger like you... supposed to put together this massive "plan" without feeling entirely overwhelmed and tasked to death? (Believe me, I know the feeling. Been there, done that.) This is a plan that has to be easy. Uncomplicated. Something you can implement within a couple hours, and not tie up your entire day on a daily basis.

First, let's have an understanding about Pinterest for the short and long game. Pinterest takes a bit to get moving. That's not a bad thing, necessarily. Anything worth doing requires time and patience.

But man, once Pinterest gets going with your pins, it's going to be nonstop traffic. I can promise you that. Why people get frustrated and confused by Pinterest is because they treat it like social media and a fleeting thing, expecting instantaneous results when it is a search engine, and is a long-term strategy.

So yes, it's going to require your patience. It's going to require effort. But the payoff is far beyond any post you can put up on social media. And, it doesn't cost a dime, unless you choose to invest in software like Tailwind.

Remember how we talked about the Pinterest smart feed? Well, it's based on these factors:

1. images
2. keywords
3. domain authority

In order to have a winning game plan, then you need to know what Pinterest likes, and doesn't like. Pinterest favors accounts with clear, beautiful images that resonate with their users. It's all about visual recognition.

Pinterest helps bloggers like you to be found through search and discovery, not through a fleeting image in posted order on Facebook, Instagram, or Twitter. This means that you need to establish a high level of domain authority. That means, the quality of content being shared from your website. Are people sharing pins from your domain? Or is your site spammy? Are you sharing a good balance of 80% other peoples' content and 20% your own? If your content is worthy of sharing, and is being re-pinned, Pinterest will reward you. If your site's pins are NOT being shared by others, and have a low re-pin rate, then Pinterest most likely will bury you, and not show your pins.

So basically, this is a game of "the pinner with the best content and pin designs wins" type game. It levels the playing field, because remember, it doesn't cost you anything to pin and have your pins shared. It DOES cost money to have your posts shown and shared on

Facebook and Twitter, with the way they've completely overhauled their systems.

This game is fair and balanced for everyone - because no matter how much money you throw at it, if your pins are not being shared or re-pinned, Pinterest will deem the pin as low-quality and not of interest to its users. Make it high-quality, and you'll win by getting re-pins, shares, and Pinterest will show your pin naturally, maybe even suggest it in an email to all its users interested in that topic. It's really that simple.

Overall, this game plan involves quality images, content, and keywords. Strike the perfect balance between all three on each and every pin, and you'll be set for incredible web traffic consistently.

Remember - you can't compare Pinterest to Instagram, Twitter, or Facebook. This is an entirely different game that you'll be playing. And it's a winning strategy for ANY blogger.

The Average Pinterest User

For your average Pinterest pinner, Pinterest is where they go to build their ideas. It is the first point of contact, but it isn't the last. They often search and discover ideas on Pinterest, either buy direct from the pinner they are most impressed by, or sign up to get more information on how to do something. This is the beauty of Pinterest. Pinterest has a higher buyer demographic than your average Facebook or Twitter user. They'll save pins for later, read them when they have time, learn how to do things, save it for future reference, and most importantly, dream.

Pinterest is full of dreamers who are doers. They love to be inspired, dream, plan, buy, and fill their lives with things they want to do and try. It's truly a wonderful platform. There's no hostility, negativity, disagreements, or social banter. They are free to do their dreaming and planning, as they see fit, without all that other stuff interrupting them.

We love the average Pinterest user. Remember that. They are going to be a big part of your game plan, and it's going to be your job to impress them with your pins.

Getting More Clicks from Pinterest

Speaking of impressing Pinterest users, you're going to get them to click over from Pinterest to your site. It's super important. Because that's how you'll get people to sign up for your email list. Impress the user with your pin, get them to your site, and get them to sign up for your email list. Then continue to wow them. Simple plan, right? Exactly. Let's focus on how to get more clicks to your website.

1. Pinnable Images – The first way to get more clicks is with great pinnable images. Long, gorgeous images. You want to be captivating, pique their interest, and lure them in with amazing content.

What makes for an engaging pinnable image? Let's answer that with another question. Why do certain billboards catch your eye more than others? Colors, text, images, numbers - these all stand out on Pinterest as people scroll through the feeds. Your images need to be bright, easy to read, captivating, the text nice and large or artistically displayed, and have a compelling reason to click through to your site.

And the easiest way to tell what's popular is... to research the most popular pins on Pinterest, use software, and emulate (don't copy) what other pinners are doing, while making your own style.

2. Keywords – Keywords rule Pinterest. They're super important because users go to the platform and type exactly what they are looking into the search bar, and drill down from there. There are two great ways to look for keywords on Pinterest. There are two ways that search functions on Pinterest: prediction, where Pinterest takes what you type into the search bar and gives you what the algorithm thinks you're interested in based on what you're typing (will list out other things people have typed in), and the other is through the guided search boxes, where Pinterest will display a submenu of keyword options and phrases that the user can pick from to further refine their search. Both are excellent tools to use for establishing your keywords in your pins, by the way.

Be sure to include your keywords in your board names as you're creating them or modifying your existing board names, because they can be indexed by Google. Using very specific board names isn't just beneficial on Pinterest, as it also gives Google more information about what your board is about.

Board descriptions, surprisingly, don't play into search in the same capacity that board names do. Board descriptions are more for telling users about what the board is about, rather than playing a big role in the function of search. So focus more on board names - actual things people would be searching for (not Things for My Dog Skippy's New Doghouse, because that's just not a board people would actually be searching for).

For a long time, we believed that boards that we weren't pinning to very often or that were outside of our niche were hurting us, but they're not, from an algorithm standpoint. What you should be focusing on is that you're pinning to boards that contain content and keywords that your audience is searching for. Just remember that the place where you are most active is where you will get the most engagement from both exposure, re-pins, and followers.

The next step for keywords is in your pin description. Keep it at one to two sentences, with a bunch of keywords in the most authentic, non-spammy way possible. Find a way to integrate the keywords using normal speech, rather than forced dialogue. Also, remember to integrate hashtags at the bottom, including your own custom branded hashtag, as they work for chronological hashtag feed.

Now Let's Grow Your Email List

So now you're going to combine images, pin descriptions and keywords all together. This is your new happy place! This is where blog visits happen. Where new readers of your blog or website or book, become subscribers. Your work will pay off. Now you've led them to your website, so now you have traffic. What you do next is completely up to you, and ultimately what dictates your success.

Sometimes, working really hard at Pinterest pays off. Within 3 months I had an email list of over 40k. 2 years later, my list is at over 90k. For others, though, depending on how niched out your blog topic is, it could take longer to reach that level of growth. But if you find something that really resonates with your audience, you can expect to have email growth like crazy. You are about to cultivate a list of people that want to know what you think, what you know, and how you're able to change their lives for the better.

I created a special opt-ins to build my list. I did it two ways. One was a free course on re-purposing content, and the other was creating a resource library where people could download some business tools like workbooks and checklists to build their blogs. I then created content upgrades for sale, put them in a sales funnel where my new subscribers could access them, and delivered quality content from that point on, delivering on my brand, which is to educate and provide resources to make things easier for bloggers.

Make sure you give an incentive for people to get and stay on your list. Keep them by constantly delivering value time and time again. Inspire them, educate, inform, create with them, and make them your people. You'll have officially found your tribe, just as I have found mine.

Put Yourself in Your Readers' Shoes

Now that you have your readers coming over to your website, it's time to start making some sales. Warm them up. Invite them into your world, and get them contemplating how their life can be easier or more creative with you involved. Lead them down a funnel where they'll discover just how valuable your knowledge is!

Make sure that you're not driving traffic to dead links. That is bad. If you have a few dead links on your page, redirect to a live page with a custom "whoopsie!" page or a page that makes it seem like they were supposed to arrive there all along. The one mistake I saw doing this was a Pinterest user who just had redirects to a home page, and it never led to an article or a replacement article.

Try to ensure that your products are placed in lifestyle shoots and appear realistic. Quality mockups, real photos with bright lighting work incredibly well here for this kind of marketing. People who peruse on Pinterest want EVERYTHING they see. They're in the mood to be inspired and take action on things they want to do.

Using Analytics to See What's Working

Now that you have your clicks, email lists, and sales, we want to evaluate whether it's all working or not. The three main places I go for analytics reporting and decision-making are Google Analytics, Pinterest Analytics, and Tailwind.

When I go to my Google Analytics report, I'm looking at what pins are driving the most traffic to my site. Pinterest and Google Analytics help me see the people I'm reaching, what they're interested in, their demographics, how long they stay, what they do on my site, which pages they end up leaving, whether they sign up for my email list and where, and more. All this data helps me figure out what my next project is, and it'll tell you, too, what you should do more of. Use all these signals to determine what to do next! The reports will guide you. They're not your enemy. Learn to love Analytics!

If you use Tailwind software, this too, can help you see how your pins are performing. You can also see how many times your particular pins have been saved, which boards are performing the best, your viral score, engagement score, and more.

Pinterest marketing will be slow-moving at first. But give it time. You can go from 80k monthly viewers to 10 million within two months. I'm living proof! And believe me - I spent a long time hovering in the 4-digit range and eventually made it into the 6-digit range within 18 months. And while there are those that say not to focus so much on the monthly viewers metric, know that it does relate to website traffic, so it's definitely a metric to watch closely - and be proud of! But the most important metric I would say is to watch your domain stats - the monthly traffic that leads people from your pins to your website. It's on the right side of the analytics page on Pinterest. Watch this carefully - and take your cues from there.

Taking Action Based on Results

So you have traffic coming in... people signing up, and you're maybe starting to make sales. A few. Or maybe none yet. Who knows!? What do you do next? Well, you look at what is performing best on your Pinterest profile, focus on your most popular boards, work them, and let Pinterest and Google tell you where you need to focus more attention for nurturing your audience. Your most popular boards will help you dictate what kind of content to continue blogging about.

Pin every single day. I use Tailwind so I'm pinning 24/7. My account grows by over 100 new followers each day, and has been going this rate since December 2018, when my blog finally took off. But the best advice I can give is find that perfect sweet spot of managing your boards, pinning frequency, and developing content that nurtures both your audience as well as your Pinterest followers.

Check your analytics weekly. (I check mine daily). If Pinterest or Google analytics are a confusing and frustrating thing for you, watch some videos, learn a little, take a class (or take my Masterclass). Invite people along with you on your Pinterest journey. Share your boards! Share your Pinterest profile and let people know what you're doing!

Be patient. Pinterest takes time. People who attempt to use Pinterest for their marketing plan and give up way too early are the same people that could be right where I'm at, 2 years later from when I first started. Never give up. You'll know you're getting close when things start to click. Just keep at it. This is not a quickie get rich quick thing AT ALL. This is truly a challenging test of how good your content is, and how good your website is, and the traffic will show you whether you're good or not. And if you're not good yet, that doesn't mean you can't become great.

Don't get discouraged. Keep trying. If you're not making sales, you're just a few small adjustments away from figuring it all out. Don't throw in the towel without first making some subtle changes to your web copy, your pins, and most importantly, getting someone's outside, objective opinion.

What Do You Do if Your Pinterest Plan Isn't Working?

Take a deep breath before you panic, if you are starting to feel like your Pinterest plan isn't working. Believe me, I've been there. There was a time where I thought that I was just going to be another voice in the wind... just another blogger with something to say, but no real audience. But at that point where you think you should give up, you might be the closest to your ultimate success.

People that get frustrated or impatient with Pinterest forget that this is a long-term haul. Sure, you might have some pins take off within a day (like I have), but know that it could take days, weeks, or even months for your pins to really gain some traction. This is not social media.

Focus on your Google Analytics and what pins are giving you the most traffic. This is the insight that will give you the heads up on what you need to focus the most on, and what your readers are most interested in. Too often, when people expect that if they do this and that, that it will equal instant success, and it doesn't happen that way, they start to panic and try anything and everything, losing sight of their end user and reader base. Don't pin to serve the algorithm. Server your readers and what is driving the traffic to your site.

Here are some hints:

1. Know your reader. Their struggles. What job titles they have.

2. Keep on creating content that servers your readers. When your audience feels like they're being served by your content, they'll share it, pin it, and save it.

3. Remember to reward your reader base with some unexpected freebies every once in a while. Give them nuggets. I know that you've spent a great deal of time prepping your products, materials, and deserve to be compensated for them. But remember to reward your readers for listening to you. They'll appreciate you even more than before. This in effect creates a loyal fan base of people who will come back to you time and time again.

Finally, think about your target audience. Who are they? Go back to your basics and make sure you're serving your core audience with things that will keep them inspired, and coming back for more.

27 HOW TO USE ANALYTICS TO CREATE BETTER CONTENT

98 percent of users go out and try the ideas they find on Pinterest.

———

Your analytics will give you an immense amount of insight on what content to create next. For example, I figured out my audience was really into Canva templates, bookstagram images, and bullet journaling. I have a plethora of writers and bloggers following me, and that it what they are predominantly into. So I create content specifically for them. So listen to your analytics and act on those results! Serve your readers and increase your income by listening to them.

What are the Common Themes of Your Most Viral Posts?

Take a look at your top 10 or top 20 posts and look for commonalities. Is there anything in common that seems to trigger a response? Is it a certain keyword phrase or product? A specific image? A topic? Look for what your audience is loving based on the metrics. This will help you learn more about your audience.

This is, in essence, going to give you buying signals. Major brands actually use Pinterest as a way to decide what to carry in their stores based on how their items are performing on Pinterest. Why create something or stock something if it's getting bad reception or zero response? Look for what people like, what they're sharing, and make more of THAT. Become an "inventory purchaser" like a department store, and choose selectively what you list in your store and write about on your site.

Selling Products on Your Site

I have created numerous products on my store that have been triggered by audience response. For example, I figured out that my email list was really interested in time-saving lead magnets. They weren't so interested in website design strategies. Which was surprising, because I'm a web designer, and thought that was why people predominantly followed me. Nope. They were into my solutions for getting more content and lead magnets out there with a designer look to them, along with my ideas for content. Who knew?! Well, I wouldn't have known that if I hadn't really evaluated my video views, my pins, and how my email list responded to my emails.

So not only did listening and watching my readers' responses benefit me financially, but it benefitted them, too, because now they have access to items that have helped ME along the way, and get a backstage pass into my blogging world. Watch what they click on. Check every email campaign report. I even watch who unsubscribes, because I have such few unsubscribes. And that's what you want - only a few unsubscribes, growth in your list, and sales emerging from your email list.

Disenchantment with Your Brand

You're going to have feelings of being redundant. Like, seriously, how many times can you say "Product X is Amazing! Check it out!" You'll feel like a broken record sometimes. But just remember, there are 230 million people on this platform that most likely have never heard of you, and it will not be new to them. If you're seeing buying signals or high interest, take that as a positive thing and run with it.

Don't let redundancy feelings deter you from success. You're here to serve them, not yourself. And while Pinterest is really fun most of the time, this is a business, and of course from time to time you're going to feel bored with the variations of pins based on the same product or topic. Stay positive, my friend.

Look for Commonalities in Images

The other way I look for triggers to see what kind of content or products to create next is to evaluate my images. Which ones perform the best? What colors, objects, and fonts getting the most results?

Here's how I evaluate images:

1) Was it flat lay, perspective, or front view?

2) Was it mostly image or did it have a box overlay with some text?

3) Did the pin image contain screenshots of a content upgrade or a lead magnet?

4) Did the pin image have big fonts or small?

5) Did the pin image have varied fonts or just one?

6) What was the pin layout?

This is one thing where you may want to use an Excel spread-sheet to conduct your evaluation with rows and columns of data so you can sort of quantify some of these things. Or, you could use a notebook and jot down your notes, with the commonalities that one dictating how you'll produce more high-performing pins.

What Keywords are Rocking Your Pins?

We specifically choose keywords as part of our overall pinning strategy. So which ones are performing the best? Check your pin descriptions. Which words or phrases did you use that seem to consistently be in each viral pin? This could be related to a topic, a hashtag, organizing, strategy, a number, anything. Knowing what your audience is interested in will help dictate your keyword use, but if you're doing Pinterest "correctly", you'll notice some commonalities there within your most popular pins. Don't forget to use your analytics keyword planner if you need help in the future deciding which keywords to use.

Create What Your Audience Loves

It's been shown even on my own blog that even the smallest products like a simple ebook packed with solid, reliable, and helpful information make for great relationships between you, the blogger, and your reader. Don't always focus on the big budget items. Smaller product nuggets work just as great, and you'll be keeping the budget-minded folks close to your heart in the process.

Summary

The main issue that bloggers tend to have (who fail) is creating things that their audience just isn't interested in. And continuing to create more and more of the same thing in hopes that they'll convert to sales. They don't listen to their audience by studying their analytics. So the biggest piece of advice I can give you is to really study your analytics and listen to your audience. Study close what they watch, what they love to download, and that will tell you EXACTLY what you need to do.

Big brands do the same thing. They don't just buy anything and everything. They make strategic purchases to serve their customer. Big brands know what their customers want, and deliver it. You are capable, even as a one-person show, to do the very same thing.

28 HOW TO MEASURE SUCCESS WITH PINTEREST KPIS

Visual searches on Pinterest have more than doubled in one year.

I'm not one for wasting time, money, or other resources to "figure things out". If there's a carrot at the end of the stick, I'll bite, if I know that it's going to improve any situation. This is where looking at your KPIs or Key Performance Indicators comes into play, because these numbers will ultimately decide what you produce, how much, what you'll charge, what you'll invest in, what you'll spend more time on, and so on.

WHAT ARE KPIS?

KPIs are data indicators measured at a specific point in time. They give us the revealing information on how our blogs and businesses are performing, and help make decisions for the future. They help us draw distinctions between profitability and cutting our losses.

These numbers could be your growth in email list, a sales conversion rate, your overall sales totals, lead magnet signups, etc. These metrics are merely a way to put a number to a measurement of an activity's overall effectiveness.

One business owners' KPIs will differ from another business, simply because businesses in different fields will have starkly different ratios and indicators. Make sure you research your industry's or niche's KPI numbers first before measuring your own business against someone else. And try not to make this evaluation process overly difficult or the equivalent of a calculus III collegiate-level class.

Once you have your numbers, focus on one segment of your business at a time, looking for improvements in that one area. Don't try to do "all the things" all at once. I say this because focusing on one segment may have a trickle-down effect into other segments of your business. For example, more subscribers might equate to more sales.

Pinterest-Specific KPIs

There are four major KPIs associated with Pinterest: re-pins, saves, views, and followers. Most people believe that there are only three major KPIs (re-pins, saves, and followers), but you'll quickly see how I make the correlation between monthly views to blog traffic.

The debate on whether or not followers is a valuable metric to measure will continue to go on. However, given that Pinterest has an exclusive "Following" button at the bottom of the app on mobile devices, as well as a tab at the top next to your profile picture, I would argue that followers still continues to be an element of Pinterest to continue to grow and measure, as I have found a mushroom effect with monthly views and clicks / re-pins happen with the gain of followers.

But first, let's start with my own metrics.

KPIs for the KerrieLegend.com

My top KPIs for my website include:

1. revenue
2. email conversions

3. number of emails in funnel prior to sale

4. overall profit/loss

5. website traffic - page views, page sessions

Revenue is obviously an important thing to measure, because money puts food on the table, puts kids in college, makes the payments, you know, #life. The second most important thing for my business is email conversion. With a list of 90k that I've built over the last few years, it's important to use the traffic that I have, discover what my readers need from me and deliver that, and convert to sales as part of all the effort that goes into building a product or resource.

The next thing I look at is the number of emails I send before I earn a sale. I have a funnel set up to deliver valuable content and resources, and I like to know how soon before someone accesses my resource library before they grab something from my shop. I also look at profit and loss, and I'm lucky in that the only losses I really experience are on Facebook ads when something doesn't "go" or "sell" like I thought it would. Hence, I've shifted my focus onto really looking at what is the most popular and most searched-for terms and pins on my site. That has helped me turn the corner from 2018 into 2019. I experienced a dramatic shift in revenue and engagement via email when I changed my focus a bit.

Then, I focus on website traffic. Ads on my website net around $500-1000 per month on my site, so it's good to have them there, paying for my time and effort in the event that I'm in creation mode and not actively pursuing a product campaign. I also focus on traffic in the sense of measuring how many page views I receive per session. I like to see at least five page views when I have a visitor. Keep in mind that your email list subscribers are likely to spend more time on your site than random visitors. You'll build your loyalty base over time as you grow your email list.

Let's Talk About Traffic...

The page view debate will continue to happen and there are various schools of thought on its importance. I think about how many sites that I discovered on Pinterest that I have become a loyal fan of. I also think about search elements and what brought me to those sites from Google. Those counted as page views, and ultimately, conversions, for those blog business owners. So to say that page views are not really important, think about how revenue from your blog is made and whether or not a sale could have been made if the user had not found your site in the first place. Right?!

Now, with ads and ad revenue on your site, more page views do not mean more ad revenue automatically. More engaged users or loyal readers will stay on your site longer, visit more pages, and will likely click on more things like ads, thus driving up ad revenue for your site.

I've also noticed that those who think that page views are a "vanity metric" are also the same people trying to make money offering Pinterest services with lower monthly page views on their Pinterest accounts than professional bloggers with over 10 million monthly views and over 400k page views and 75k user sessions. Of course, revenue per page is a good metric to use, but not every single page needs to be a product push, as some people will lead you to believe. Overselling is never a good trait on any site.

It's good, rather, to think of all these metrics as equally important, as each focus area has its benefits and rewards, along with costs. To me, revenue is just as important as reader loyalty. Because if you don't have loyal readers, you won't have incoming revenue from trusting fans, either. And I LOVE my readers. I love Freebie Friday and making their day, and hopefully you can find something applicable to reward your readers, too.

What is the End Goal with Ads?

I don't throw money away on ads. I always have an end goal in mind. Typically, it's a sales conversion. And even though I do very well financially with my blog (over $3 million in sales in 3 years) it still wrenches my gut to give Facebook any ad revenue for zero conversion. The same with LinkedIn, Twitter, Instagram, et al. Even $42 spent on a Facebook ad with no end result is terrible for me.

Perhaps it's my frugal mentality, and thinking that money could have gone to my kids in some fashion.

The only place where I actually saw improvement on my blog with ANY ad, was with Pinterest. For reals. And if you think about it, Pinterest is really a playground for "ads" - pins with content upgrades available, freebies, products, etc. But it really doesn't feel that way because it's all beautiful visuals. This is a playground for people who WANT to be approached with new ideas, products, and who want to learn and plan to do new things.

So let's say you spend $100 on an ad - Facebook, Pinterest, or elsewhere. And you get maybe 30% conversion. You'll track how many people signed up for your email list, and then how many people you were able to convert. Tweak your website a little, maybe adjust your email a bit, and you'll have higher conversion. This is all about a game of testing, tweaking, paying, testing, tweaking and paying.

The two things you're going to have to watch is your cost per lead and your cost per conversion. With algorithms on each platform changing regularly, it's difficult to gauge how much you'll end up spending each month should they integrate a change. Know what your ideal return is before you take out your ad.

I generally give ads three chances after tweaking and modifying to start either converting or performing. Watch your relevancy rank with Facebook ads as that will dictate how often your ads are shown and whether or not the audience you're targeting is even interested in what your message is. After a day or so, you'll know what your per-click cost is going to be, so be sure you're comfortable with that number before you commit to hundreds of dollars on ads.

Revenue Metrics

What is a good cost per lead? It varies based on industry and the blog, as well as what you're selling on your site. If your site is filled to the brim with affiliate links, those sales may very well pay for your ad spend. So driving traffic with a $.75 click that nets a $1.00 affiliate link income makes sense. Or if you know that a specific Google Adsense ad that is on your leaderboard constantly gets a $1.75 click, and you're driving traffic to that page for $.35, it makes sense to make revenue on that page.

Where you can really go bonkers and have fun is if you also make money on something you SELL on that page, too. Do some testing and duplicate the page and see what happens! I do A/B testing all the time (my audience just doesn't see me doing it).

What I would recommend is using a plugin called Pretty Links, where you can mask and track your affiliate links and see how they're converting - how many clicks, for example. It'll help keep your site nice and neat.

How Do I Start Blogging to Make Money with Pinterest?

Staring out will seem overwhelming at first. Take it in steps. I would recommend writing consistently and work on your lead magnets first, before introducing them. Fill your blog with content and have things organized first. Quality content and upgrades do in fact get shared. So start building something you can be proud of first - this applies whether you're an author, blogger, crafter, whatever. We're all doing the same function, just different content.

Also, site design plays a BIG part in whether or not you'll make money from your site. The majority of authors I know simply haven't invested in their sites enough and struggle with sales as a result. Beginning bloggers often try to take cheaper shortcuts that bring on painful side effects like lack of options, domain transfer locks for periods of time, overspending on monthly 3ʳᵈ party fees instead of self-hosting, instead of working with a web designer straight out to get things right the first time. This is all wasted time and effort. If you really want to nail your blog down and get moving fast, hire a graphic designer. It'll be the MOST important investment you'll make. You don't want people closing out of your site just because it's not pleasing to the eye.

Pinterest is an interesting network and community of people, and you'll find your material gets re-pinned by people who are offering the same thing you are, and that is because we view, as a community of users, other peoples' content just as valuable to our audience as our own. It's a completely different, non-competitive network of bloggers that I think you'll really enjoy.

Keep Your Options Open

You may find the need to shift your product line, your focus areas, and topics as you start seeing trends in the consumption of your pins and content. What you thought would be popular may not be. Or perhaps technology changes and your product is no longer relevant. Again, listen to your analytics and go with what it's saying (more like screaming).

Get to the point where people know you. You want people responding to your emails. You want transparency and honesty with your audience. It's not just about creating great products, broadcasting them, taking out ads, and hoping for sales. You really need to figure out what is the most meaningful to your audience. That takes time. And you may have to adjust.

And it's not all about web traffic. It doesn't pay for your cell phone bill. Income does. But you do need traffic in order to make income. Remember that.

29 ETSY SHOPS, ONLINE STORES, AND BOUTIQUES

Pinterest is the fastest growing website by overall member growth.

Suppose you have products listed in your store that are either one-of-a-kind or even limited in quantity. And you sell out. What about those pins that you created for those products? Do you delete them? What about the pins that are other boards you don't own?

You'll still have incoming traffic to those links. And certainly, you don't want your visitors to get 404 errors when coming to your website.

So... what's the answer to this little predicament?

If possible, try redirecting to a similar product with an indication that the original product is no longer available or in stock, but they might enjoy this particular product or item instead.

Or, you could always offer a "hey, sorry this isn't available, but here's a discount code to use on another item".

It's not possible to mass update pins on Pinterest. You can only update and edit the pins YOU have created and saved on your boards.

If anything else, try using a custom 404 page that redirects the user's attention to what IS available and hopefully you'll still be able to secure them as a client or customer, or at the very least, a subscriber.

Using Pinterest Without Writing a Blog

Some people want to make money off of Pinterest without actually blogging, and want to know if it's possible. It is, but you're talking about affiliate income trickling in. I would recommend at least building an email list and building a relationship with your followers on Pinterest by communicating with them through your newsletters and email campaigns.

I believe that blogging is a better buffer to introduce people to affiliate links, and gives your site much more personality, but it IS possible to use Pinterest and make money off of it without actually writing.

How to Get it ALL Done

I use an editorial calendar. On busy months, I stick to blogging once a week in long-form blogging. In less busy months, or in months where I can really crank out content that I've been working on, I can blog daily. I spend 4 hours a week blogging and pinning combined.

Once you have your blog headlines figured out (filled with keywords, hopefully), develop your planned list of keywords and hashtags.

One or two days after posting, check your analytics and see how your pins are performing. Are they a hit? Some of my pins have become so popular within one day that they reached 7.k-9k people in a matter of hours... just because of the title on the pin and the related keywords.

Is it Possible to Climb the Ranks on the Smart Feed?

Pin descriptions and board descriptions, as well as how often your pin is clicked and saved, will determine how you climb the ranks. Make sure you're not just filling descriptions with a bunch of keywords. Use full sentences - three to five of them full of keywords. You can integrate four to six hashtags, as well.

Multiple Sites?

Let's say you have two blogs to manage... or more. Give each one equal attention. Keep each one branded, and only overlap and inter-link the two of them when it's appropriate or the content is similar. You'll be able to manage both accounts from Tailwind, but you'll only need to pay for tribes for the one, because you can share pins from the other account using your main account with the upgraded tribes access.

What Works, and What Doesn't

• Board covers do matter when people look through your whole account. You can stick with simple images and text, and get along just fine.

• Do not waste your time following and unfollowing. That is for losers.

• Don't get cute or overly generic with your board titles using words that no one would search for. Many authors make the mistake of doing work in progress boards and have them on display for readers to possibly see. From a search standpoint, they serve absolutely no value other than to yourself. For bloggers, sometimes they get cute with weird titles or add symbols and unnecessary character breaks in them. Don't do that. This is search-oriented. People are not going to search for "where I want to go this year". They'll be searching for things like "Disney travel recommendations" or "resorts", etc. Use board titles like that which are searchable and specific.

• Followers matter. Do let your readers know they can find you on Pinterest. You can now choose the *"Explore feed"*, which will search topics, or the *"Follower feed"*, which will only show you pins from the people or boards you follow.

Buyable Pins

Buyable pins are available for people using Shopify and BigCommerce. It has a "Buy Now" button on it, and lets people checkout inside Pinterest without leaving the platform.

This is something that is still an adjustment for Pinterest users, but it is growing. I foresee more and more platforms that compete with Shopify and BigCommerce to join in on the buyable pin algorithm. It's only a matter of time.

Promoting Pins

I only run promoted pins when I want to test a product for interest before I send it to my email subscribers. Based on the level of interest and reach, I'll make the decision whether to launch or not, or just let the new product sit on my site and probably collect a few sales initially.

Have a game plan in mind for your strategy and expectations on how you want the promotion to perform. What would be a successful conversion rate for you? Or, you could use promoted pins to get new email subscribers to your site.

Local Businesses Without E-Commerce

Can you use Pinterest for local business without e-commerce opportunities? Is it possible to optimize for local business? Yes.

Pinterest will eventually recognize, after enough hashtags and locale mentions in your pin descriptions, that you are targeting that specific location. This is most helpful if you have a board dedicated to your topic with the city and state referenced. In every single pin description, use a keyword indicating your location. Be abundantly clear and specific about your location by including the state as well.

30 HOW TO DO A/B TESTING ON PINTEREST IMAGES

Pins aren't seen as ads...even when they are.

Get more mileage out of your content by creating more images and pins for your content. Test the images and pins by using A/B testing. You'll be able to quickly discern which images work better, which pin titles work better, or what keywords work better than others. Remember, images are the one thing that people see in their feed, so it's important to test what people visually like and search for, and ultimately, make more of THAT.

Don't Test More than One Variable at a Time

When testing pins, only change one variable at a time when creating a similar pin leading to the same content. Did you know that text on the image that matches the keywords can increase your conversion? And perhaps one set of keywords or phrases will perform better than another set. You won't know unless you conduct some pin testing.

Image Size

A/B testing is important. Look at what's trending and performing well. You want to know what your followers want. Size preferences and dimensions for the platform seem to be changing regularly, so it's important to vary them in size - this is how we figured out that Pinterest isn't exactly embracing the square images from Instagram like we initially thought they would.

And of course, Pinterest isn't going to give you a dimension warning trigger, they just won't show your pin. So testing dimension is essential here to find out what the algorithm likes and does not like. For example, don't exceed 1500 pixels, because your pin will get cut off. I believe the new recommendation is no longer than 1260 pixels in length or it won't be shown on the mobile feeds anymore.

And remember that just because something is working for another Pinner's account doesn't mean it'll work brilliantly for yours. You have distinct audiences with different tastes. Take the time to test and learn, and you'll notice your own unique trend happening within your own account.

Pinterest Descriptions

Pinterest has stated that it's perfectly acceptable to have multiple pins that lead to the same website page. In fact, it's beneficial to have a variety of images that might appeal to various types of pinners. But they do recommend adding unique descriptions that are specific to each pin, as it'll help SEO.

Here's how to do this. Start out with image A and B, and description 1 and 2, and then follow these steps:

1. Pin image A with description 1.
2. Then, pin image B with description 2.
3. Then, pin image A with description 2.
4. Finally, pin image B with description 2.

It doesn't matter which order you pin them in, just as long as you're developing four images for the same website page in with the above-mentioned variations.

Promoted vs. Organic Pins

With promoted pins, you'll have more control and data on

whether or not your pin is trending and picking up speed. With organic pins, there are a lot of unknowns still in play. The algorithm will determine whether or not to show your pin. One is not necessarily better than the other; you just have more control and data feedback with promoted pins.

UTMs

UTMs are a custom URL that you can use to track individual pieces of content via Google Analytics. You can use UTMs to differentiate and track various images.

If you use UTMs, then the unknowns on an organic pin disappear. If your pin gets picked up by someone, that UTM will stay exactly the same. When you go into your Google Analytics, you can determine the image that gets the clicks. The UTM sorts the unreliable data from hardcore data. UTMs allow you to know exactly how the image is working. Setting one up takes about 30 seconds to a minute.

Promoted Pin A/B Tests

Pinterest added *"in ad groups"* to the promoted pins campaign. This gives the pin promoter a useful place to conduct A/B testing because you could add multiple images directly into the ad group. Theoretically, you could monitor impact on the dashboard, but alas, it's not possible.

Adding more than three to five images to an ad group can cause all your ads to suffocate and die. As your ad ages, Pinterest will hook on to one image and you'll be getting zero impressions and clicks on your other images. This is a Pinterest issue, not an issue with your ad. They are aware of it and how the platform impacts those other images, but currently it's not a pressing issue for them to fix.

If you're going to use the ad groups, only use three to five images and check them regularly. Make sure you're not wasting your time and money and check their performance.

31 HOW TO SELL MORE BOOKS WITH PINTEREST

On Average 1 pin gets 11 re-pins and generates 6 website visits.

William th the emergence of the KDP platform and the wide acceptance of self-publishing, we're seeing an inflow of new authors and writers from all walks of life, experience, topics, and even some developing sub-genres. It's exciting! But with the market flooding with books and authors with little marketing experience if any, it's easy to get lost in the shuffle.

Is it possible to sell more books with Pinterest? Maybe even sell more books off your website than on Amazon, iTunes, Google Play, Kobo, etc. combined? Yes.

A couple years ago, I saw some writing on the wall with Amazon and where it was headed. The platform was ripe with fraud - fraudulent reviews, bought bestseller ranks, reviews being stricken from books, questionable KDP payouts and bonus program issues, and the list goes on. As an author community, we had placed too much power into the hands of giants, where much of the royalty revenue stayed, instead of being placed into the hands of the authors themselves.

I made the decision to remove a bunch of my titles from the KU (Kindle Unlimited) program, keeping only a fleet of them niched for certain markets available for the KU platform. I then started marketing my books off of my own website, using a few different selling platforms like Etsy, Gumroad, and Selz to sell my books and accompanying materials. Since I made that decision, I have sold many more books off my own website thanks to Pinterest than I have on Amazon and all the other publishing platform giants combined.

And with bloggers creating eBooks to sell and market, I figured I would be missing a big Pinterest topic if I didn't talk about the book market and how to sell more books with Pinterest.

What Should You Put on Your Pinterest Account?

But first, let's talk about the kinds of boards you'll want to have on your Pinterest account. Because the biggest mistake I see a lot of authors making is pinning about themselves and their books only, and hardly ANY content that their readers will actually be interested in.

For example, WIP boards. These are not board titles Pinterest users will be searching for. These really have no relevance in existing other than to give yourself inspiration for your book. I would make these boards secret instead.

Boards I would include would be your own board with your author name, your genre name (i.e., Non-Fiction Books, Romance Books / Novels, etc.), reading memes, book memes, reading nooks, writer things, writing tools, interesting libraries, home office inspiration, recipes that go along with your books, book swag, or anything you think your readers would be interested in, etc. Be sure to share others you compete with on your Pinterest boards - with 80% being other authors, and 20% of your own material.

Too often, I run into author Pinterest accounts that have been "ghosted" by Pinterest, because the author made the mistake of pinning too much from their own site and not enough from other pinners. You have to remember that pinning is a community sharing opportunity, not a platform that is all about you. It's about discovering new titles with your book being one of the options, not a portfolio platform. If you think you've been ghosted by Pinterest, start pinning other peoples' content and watch and wait for your numbers to climb before your start pinning from your own domain again. Pinterest needs to see your account pinning other content than just your own.

There are three areas that I think are relevant to cover related to marketing a book on Pinterest: ARC teams, book cover images vs. bookstagram images, and finally, lead magnet pins.

ARC Teams

One of the most popular search terms on Pinterest is the word "free". Combine that with "book" and obviously you have "free book". There is a population of readers on Pinterest who will gladly read and review your books if you give them an advance reader copy. This is one of the best ways to grow an ARC team, outside of posting and asking readers on social media to join or download your ARC teams. As pins have a much longer lifespan that standard social media posts, you'll find that the stream of incoming requests to join your ARC team will be much more consistent and ongoing and much less spike-oriented like social media can be.

A healthy sprinkling of consistent pins, put on a loop rotation, to invite readers in to join your ARC team or author fan club is all it takes. Soon enough, you'll have an arsenal of readers you can count on to help you launch your books. It's how I've built mine, in conjunction with asking my email list to sign up.

Growing your ARC team on Pinterest makes sense as bigger teams will net you more reviews during your launch week, and you certainly don't want to exhaust your existing followers on social media by repetitive requests to join your ARC team or read an advanced copy. With Pinterest, you'll reach a much wider audience and tap into readers you might not have reached with your social media accounts. I would most definitely go wide with your pins here to build an ARC team.

Book Cover Images vs. Bookstagram

During the course of the three months of studying and testing how to grow on Pinterest, I did some testing on book marketing on Pinterest. What I discovered was quite interesting. Traditionally, we've uploaded book covers to Pinterest and linked them to either our websites or to Amazon. But I found that these boards filled with book covers and collections of book covers with a similar theme were not as popular or viral as the boards with bookstagram images. Bookstagram images outperformed standard book covers by over 1000% on my account. I tested similarities on 10 other accounts, and the results were similar.

So my recommendation, if you want to be seen more on Pinterest and saved to more boards, invest in bookstagram images or flat lays of your books. High-quality images; not ones you've taken from your phone and uploaded. There is most definitely a standard to the book-stagram photo movement, and I would recommend either reviewing my Bookstagram board on Pinterest or following a bunch of Insta-gram accounts of bookstagrammers to see the quality of photos.

It's important mix a combination of pin links to both your selling platforms and your website. Never post promotional material related to your book on Pinterest, like giveaways, sales, and such. Pinterest is for evergreen and long-term content. Permanent material and content.

Here's where things get really interesting, though. A lot of the bookstagrammers are sharing their images on Pinterest, but not including a link back to any website. So when you go into Tailwind to schedule these pins and images, because they're amazing, Tailwind won't share it without a link. So what I did was include the images on a bookstagram-dedicated page on my website, and included that link there.

So when they click through on the bookstagram images, they'll arrive on my site, which has a bunch of bookstagram images and bookstagram resources. If the visitor is into bookstagram images and and making them, or even books to read, they'll be able to check out my mockup sets as well as my own books. Within the page I have a

Pinterest board with all the bookstagram images that people can check out within a widget from the Pinterest platform.

Provided you use a Pinterest widget, you can highlight bookstagrammers' pins on your site and share the books and works of others while at the same time, promoting yourself and pinners that visit your site to learn more about what you write.

To sell books off your website, you can either get a merchant account (lots of hassle sometimes), or you can get a 3rd party processor like Gumroad, Selz, or Etsy that will do the bulk of the work for you. All you have to do is give your visitors an obvious reason to buy direct from you instead of a platform like Amazon. That could be a thing with better pricing, encouraging your visitors to buy direct from the author and cut out the middle man, or provide a bonus like I do when they buy a book from the site. For example, on my site, they can download not just the book but the accompanying workbook to my nonfiction titles. This has worked GREAT for me.

If you're outside of the nonfiction market, you can include book club discussion lists that accompany the book, character sheets, bonus materials, and more. Remember that it's all about using your imagination on what you have or could create that will give them a compelling reason to buy from you instead of a large giant. People are moving away from Amazon and have grown tired of their policies and their review systems, anyway. So be sure to capitalize on those opportunities you have to convert buyers direct on your site.

Lead Magnet Pins

You might be wondering how to get book sales using lead magnet pins. And it might be a new concept for you, so let's break it down.

Lead magnets are used to get an email address in exchange for something. For you, as a writer or a blogger with an ebook, this could be an excerpt, a reading order list, a checklist of all your books available, a free chapter, a free introductory book, access to a VIP reader club, etc. Anything you have as a digital asset to exchange may work as a lead magnet item.

So in your pin design you would pose questions or calls to

actions, such as "If you like romance, you don't want to miss out on this book!" Or "Download this book if you love ___" and then insert a name of the book or the name of the author.

One particular pin concept is to if/then pins, where you put "If you loved ___ the you'll love ___." You'll put the respective book covers under each headline area. The reason why we do this is to pair more popular books that people recognize with books that they might not be familiar with (yours). You can then lead the pinner back your site, have them sign up, download a book (preferably one they buy), and let them check out your site. Hopefully by now you've invested some time in making adjustments so that your site is impressive to bring the pinner back to your site for more. Also, be sure that you're putting out new and interesting content that supports or creates interest in some of your backlist.

THE KEY here is that Pinterest is not for YOU. It's for your readers (both current and prospective) and what search terms they use to find new books to read, along with what you have to offer to keep them entertained and informed. Shift your focus on your readers and what they want to learn, read, or know about, and your Pinterest account will start to grow.

32 80K TO 14+ MILLION MONTHLY VIEWS IN 3 MONTHS

"Pinning is aspirational, which means that data on pins is data on people's aspirations." - Robert Moore

A s I mentioned in the foreword, December 2018 was a major shift for me and my blog. I had been using Pinterest for about 2 years, really studying it, focusing my attention on it, but really wasn't getting anywhere "extreme" with it, traffic-wise.

I was stuck with my follower count - around 4k or thereabouts. Growing, but only maybe by 3 people a day. I pinned regularly, uploaded my blog content, pinned great materials, and was growing my email list just fine. But my traffic wasn't where I really knew it could be. Don't get me wrong - Pinterest at any level of traffic is going to be helpful. But what if you really wanted your blog to rock?

Was I going to be just another blogger with a little traffic and a few loyal followers forever? Ugh.

I was beyond frustrated, honestly. I had steady income, a good amount of followers and readers on my email newsletter, but the one thing I was missing was the major traffic that a blogger with THAT size of an email list should have. For a few moments, I felt pathetic. I had been working at Pinterest so hard for so long. And yes, it had rewarded me with so much. But why was my blog so lacking in heavy traffic and instead just getting mediocre traffic?

Seeing accounts with 10 million monthly views, I had to wonder how they got to that point. I set a small goal of 1 million monthly views just to see if I could get there. And with Pinterest, you have to be careful with spamming content and such, so the answer isn't just "pin a bunch of pins from your domain and wham you'll see traffic". Because that doesn't work. Each pin needs to have a strategy behind it. Spamming Pinterest with a bunch of miscellaneous crap and blog posts from your website is not the answer.

Let's talk about the monthly viewers number for a second. Your monthly viewer reach is a part of your overall reach on the platform, which has the ability to be a huge number, given there are over 230 million Pinterest users. It represents the number of possible readers that can see your pins in their smart feeds which could mean more traffic being directed to your site. With an increase in monthly views, there is theoretically an increase in your domain page views. That's why that number matters and why it's so significant. Some "experts" say that number doesn't matter, but oh, it does. That's your reach number. If you see high numbers in monthly views combined with a high amount of actvitiy and views from the domain side (right column), you'll know that bloggers has Pinterest mastered, and they're active.

So I did what most people do. I started reading, in the first days of December, a ton of different blog posts. It was all the same lame, vague advice. I fell down the rabbit hole of vague ambiguity. The cesspool of the blogging world. Pin good images. Use good keywords. Yeah, I already did all that. I had the sales already, but they could always improve. I had the email list already. How many times have you sat there, reading like 425 blog posts, trying to figure something out, and apply all the advice you read, and you STILL don't get results? Yeah. Been there. All this advice on Pinterest from pinners with less than 100k in monthly views. I was not interested at all in those accounts.

I wanted the skinny on the BIG accounts... but none of the big accounts talked about how they got big on Pinterest. Silence.

Thoroughly frustrated with the thought of just being another blogger out there who was unsuccessful with yet another platform, I buckled down, determined to figure out everything. I looked at other blogs, but many were in the same boat I was with around 80k to 150k monthly viewers. Several were pinning things like "How I got 400k page views in one month from Pinterest", but gosh, that must have been a while ago, because as I looked at their Pinterest account, they were consistently at less than 200k monthly views, which meant that their domain pinning authority and traffic would be less than that. Your monthly viewers number that shows on your Pinterest profile will never be less than the amount of traffic to your website. So either they had gotten that traffic a while back and just didn't keep up with it, or they got it with a promoted pin stint.

Either way, I needed to figure out how to get more traffic so I could get more subscribers to grow even more, so I could sell more off of Pinterest directly without taxing my email list so much.

On day three of scouring all these sites for the answer (and believe me, it wasn't out there), I stopped reading other blogs. No one had the answer or was sharing it publicly. I was on my own.

It was time to test a few things. All I did was sit there in front of my laptop... for a moment of clarity. Thinking about all I had done for the past two years and what could possibly be the answer to my perplexing issue. I needed organic traffic from Pinterest without spending money on ads.

The Light Bulb Moment

Then, I had a light bulb moment. If I was already pinning great stuff, using great images and keywords, and was getting the conversion, but just not the traffic I wanted in the hundreds of thousands, then my problem or challenge wasn't really my materials. It was the amplification issue. I needed to change my amplification methods... not blog more or use different images or keywords.

And this isn't something other pinning bloggers talk about - amplification. Pinning more, quality content more frequently, according to the 10 Pinterest accounts I tested, does in fact ramp up your monthly viewers and followers, provided you have great boards and content happening, which I did.

The key here is that it is theoretically "easy" to get to 10 million monthly viewers. Watch out for the people that ONLY post that metric and brag about it without revealing their domain pinning results. For me, it varies between 400k-500k monthly views (shown in my course and in my YouTube videos), which has translated to an average of 450k page views per month, and about 75k user sessions. All people have to do to get to 10 million monthly viewers is pin a really popular pin and it'll go viral for a couple months, and really boost those numbers. They could even have zero traffic to their domain in the right column for that matter. It doesn't even have to be one of their own pins to get to that level. It is most likely someone else's that has taken off in a wild fashion. When looking at Pinterest analytics, what really matters in conjunction with the overall monthly viewers is your domain's monthly views and individual pins.

I Increased My Pinning Frequency

The first thing I changed was my pinning frequency. I went from 80 pins a day to 200. Within a couple days, I noticed my follower count increasing daily. After 15 days of pinning at 200 a day, I went to 350 pins a day. Instant results. I started getting 80-100 new followers a day. So that got figured out really quick.

Lesson learned - pinning frequency does impact follower increase per day. It also brought up my monthly viewers and profile views.

I Pushed Products that Matched My Most Popular Boards

The next thing I did was really look at my boards and virality scores via my Tailwind account. I listened to my pin audience and what they were into. I started focusing my pinning strategy on my more viral, popular boards, and pinned about 75% of my new pins to those boards. That brought my monthly viewers and profile views per month up big time. I hit 1 million monthly viewers before the end of December as a result. And we celebrated big.

I kept pushing. My new goal was to reach that coveted 10M mark, where Pinterest stops showing any number larger than that.

Now that I knew what my pin followers were into, I started creating downloadable products and books based on that content. For example, I have a really popular Bullet Journaling board, so I created bullet journal products and integrated those into my boards. Success. More sales.

The next board I looked at was my Bookstagram board. It was performing much better than my standard book cover boards from Romance Novels or other genres I have on my account. Interesting, right? So that triggered me to pin more images of my books that led back to my website instead of just the covers. Score. More sales than before, and my Amazon sales also increased, as well. By the end of February, I was at 14 million monthly viewers.

Lesson learned - tailoring your content to your most popular boards will help you amplify and make more sales... even when the most popular boards are not what you thought would be the most popular. But, if you're niching your blog and Pinterest account well, you should be able to switch gears at any moment and cater to your Pinterest audience with ANYTHING in your content arsenal.

I Listened to My Analytics

The third board I looked at was my blogging board, and how to really increase my content there to appeal to the blogger and writing community (my audience), while increasing clicks back to my website. I started pinning 20% of my own content, and put it on a smart loop, and set the integral to 2 days between re-posting to other applicable boards. So with doing that I set up consistent streaming to my website just by spacing out the same pin to different boards, and then having it on pin rotation or loop.

One of the biggest things I realized that while I was posting my content, I wasn't posting ENOUGH of my own content. So I amplified the number of pins from my own domain that I was pinning. I did a physical tally of how many pins of my own I was pinning and I was WAY under what I should have been at. So I started pinning MORE from my own domain to accompany the other 80% of others that I was pinning.

To do this, I used a software called Tailwind, just as I've used for the past couple of years. If you watch in my videos on YouTube how I pin efficiently on Pinterest using the Tailwind Chrome extension, you'll see that this is the fastest way to get your account moving and shaking while giving your readers quality content. Tailwind has also allowed me to pin around the clock without having to be actively pinning around the clock. Everything I pin is pre-scheduled and dated for release. It releases the pins I want to be seen at peak times and routinely gets new followers from around the world, when the Australians and UK pinners are most active.

I recommend taking a course on Pinterest.

Even if it's not my course (which is reasonably priced and much more in-depth than all the others), take a course on Pinterest if you want to see things in action and get the behind-the-scenes look on things. Sometimes visual learning works better for some people. In addition, you'll have access to my workbook that walks you through all the steps required to get the traffic you've been blogging so hard to get.

But first, a question. How many times have you invested in a course that you just didn't take the time to learn? I see it all the time. Students signing up, paying for courses, but never getting through the materials. I have several of them, unfortunately. If they would only take the time to learn and implement, they'd be so much better off. Be sure that when you invest in something like a Pinterest course, that you take the time and make the effort to do the work. It'll pay off. There is so much waiting for you to discover with this platform, and you'll be leaving traffic and sales on the table if you don't learn this.

(This applies to you if you skipped through the whole book just to get to this chapter).

Suppose you want to take a class on Pinterest. Would you take a class from someone who has 10 million or more monthly viewers, which signals their ability to get reach, or from some newbie blogger offering a class because they just discovered how awesome Pinterest is (and that someone told them they can make money off of courses)? The answer is pretty obvious. There are a zillion courses out there being offered by bloggers who have minuscule amounts of blog traffic from Pinterest, but have yet to really master Pinterest. Simply because they know offering courses is a money-maker. But frankly, they don't have the numbers to be ethically offering a Pinterest course. They haven't figured out how to conquer Pinterest. There's even a course that has been featured on Forbes and THAT blogger hasn't even hit the 1 million mark. That's fronting, and I know a ton of people that have taken that course that have not succeeded with Pinterest or blogging, and are STILL trying to figure out how to climb in traffic and grow their email lists effectively.

Luckily, you have this hot book in your hands with the details on what it took to get to the top. Without ads. All organic.

The one thing that Pinterest experts (and there are several) will tell you as well as pro bloggers will say, is that you can't hack together 312 pieces of advice from various blogs and expect your new "system" to work. It just doesn't work that way. Learn the whole thing top to bottom from someone with proven numbers and success (and on Pinterest, this is not something you can buy or fake like other platforms). Or, do your own testing and invest time into learning, as I've done.

Pinterest is something that you can learn in a couple of hours (just like the length of time it took you to read this book). And with anything, when you have a person speaking about their experiences in their videos often times they share stories and bits of insights that you may not be able to derive in a book, as I have done with several of my own videos. So if this is something, after reading up on Pinterest, that you want to pursue, you're invited to take my course or anyone's course on Pinterest - just look for an account that has 10 million or more monthly viewers and over 400k proven page views and 75k user sessions. These are the real pros at blogging and we, as a blogging collective, know what we're doing, and you'll be sure to see success with the right kind of advice beyond the vague and repetitive noise out there in the blogosphere.

You can do this. Now that you know the path I took, you'll be able to do it faster. So now you just have to implement.

33 CONCLUSION & CLOSING NOTES

Active pinners watch less TV and read fewer magazines.

I really hope that you have enjoyed learning more about Pinterest and developing a strategy around it to grow your blog and business. Pinterest is such a powerful tool and I know that if you implement what you learned in this book, you will be immensely successful as a blogger, writer, marketer, and entrepreneur.

Thank you for reading the book and be sure to share it with others that are not avid pinners (yet)!

Be sure to check out my other books available to you on Amazon as well as my website. My goal is to educate you with the finest of details so you have the whole story behind how something works - and not just vague information that really gets you nowhere!

If you ever need help with anything, please let me know. I'm just an email away at kerrielegend.com. If you found this book useful, please do me a favor and leave a positive review on Amazon. It's greatly appreciated to see reviews as an independent author who has chosen the path of self-publishing to see people enjoying my writing, my blog, and who benefit from my courses.

———————

YOU'RE an amazing rockstar for reading this book, and I wish you the very best!

~ Kerrie Legend ~

www.kerrielegend.com

Kerrielegend@gmail.com

34 ABOUT THE AUTHOR

K errie Legend has an undying love for the deep sea, sailing, traveling in their fifth wheel campers, raising goats, farming, and raising her family of six boys alongside her husband of over 10 years. She is an avid writer and blogger at kerrielegend.com, a site for bloggers and writers to learn and understand social media strategy. She is a course presenter and online educator.

As a graphic designer, Kerrie works full-time from home for entrepreneurs designing graphics, while homeschooling her boys. She is a proud supporter of homeschooling education, spends her days teaching bright minds, and engaging in playful dinosaur adventures with Legos and Thomas the Train.

She and her husband also (sometimes) blog at Mancave Mayhem (www.mancavemayhem.com), a site for interior design and shopping ideas for building the ultimate shecave or mancave. Her husband works full-time from home in the farming & trucking industries, and at home serves as the family carpenter, designing furniture and home solutions from repurposed wood resources. She also runs a lifestyle blog at LifeingHard.com, and blogs on her personal blog about raising

young   humans   that   are   all   "rainbow   babies"   at
RainbowBabyKids.com.

Printed in Great Britain
by Amazon